Table of Contents

CW00502281

From the Editor:

Embracing Mythos

Dear readers,

      Finding, and subsequently embracing, the mythic tradition of Europe is something that I look back on now as an integral part of my own personal journey. It was not simply a passing interest. Mythology was not just something cool, trendy, or in any other way a fad. In fact, my inclination, based on years of mainstream ideological training, had been to be dismissive of mythology.

      My American Christian upbringing had taught me to disparage the indigenous beliefs of my European forebears. Subsequent academic schooling droned into my head a kind of lofty vantage point which saw such things as mythology and folklore as the quaint beliefs of peasants and uneducated folk. It took a self-guided de-programming campaign on my part to learn to break from the ethno-masochism imposed by those who rule Western society and begin to view our indigenous heritage with new eyes.

      Once I began to embark on this path, one that might well be described as a fairytale heroine's journey, new worlds began to be revealed. Teachers presented along my path. Tests and challenges had to be met and overcome. And, I found that the life I had once known began to drift into the recesses of my memory. For, I was no longer hypnotized and lulled into a blurry half-conscious perception of reality. The reality that now lays before me is far more vivid, far more magical, and far more dangerous than that which I had known in my naïveté.

      What I know now is that monsters do lurk in the shadows, but helpers arise just when you need them. That life can feel soul-crushing, but inner strength infused with life-force from the beyond fuels our every step forward. What I now understand more clearly than ever before, is that Middle Earth is as real as J.R.R. Tolkien portrayed it. And, Mordor does, indeed, encroach. Therefore, awakening to the wisdom, insight, knowledge, and most importantly, spiritual guidance found in our own indigenous ethnic mythos is more crucial than ever.

      Today, as an ethnic group, we Europeans must look to other cultural groups who have made ethnic protectionism a priority. The obvious example that comes to mind are the cultures found in East Asia. Their mythos is largely intact. These are people who know who they are, who are rooted in their ancestral traditions, and who honor their forebears. All people worldwide would do well to look East to see what cultural preservation looks like and then apply their techniques at home.

      With this publication, my wish is to give Westerners that which Easterners have never lost: a deep understanding of self and a grounding in our own ethnic worldview. All people in the world deserve this precious gift.

Sincerely,

Carolyn Emerick

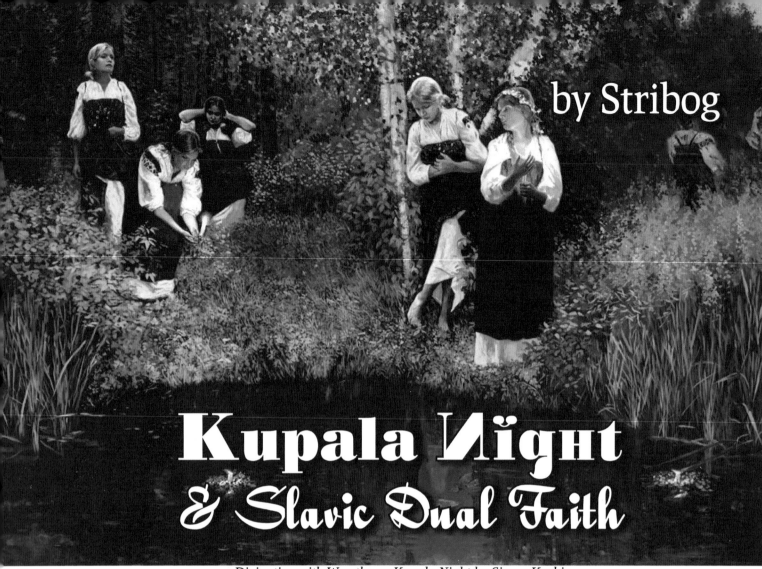

by Stribog

Kupala Night
& Slavic Dual Faith

Divination with Wreaths on Kupala Night by Simon Kozhin

The Slavic peoples of Eastern Europe are a famously strong cultural group, having retained a sense of identity (fitting neither into the traditional notions of "West" or "East") despite foreign invaders and ideologies trying to uproot and supplant the native culture and traditions for centuries. One such foreign ideology that tried to supplant native Slavic traditions and religion was Christianity, which has officially been the religion of the Slavs since 988 C.E. upon the baptism of Vladimir the Great, ruler of the Kievan Rus' (the predecessor kingdom to many Slavic countries including Russia, Belarus, and Ukraine).

Although the official state religion was Christianity, the common people for centuries retained their pagan beliefs or simply "adopted" Christianity by adding in a Christian figure instead of a pagan god and keeping all else the same, thereby escaping some scrutiny from the Orthodox clergy. Since total resistance to foreign influence is not always possible – especially if a foreign religion such as Christianity becomes official by state edict – many pre-Christian societies in Europe adopted Christianity (or other foreign ideologies) in name only, making the cultural shift either purely nominal or incredibly slow-paced. Compared to most other cultural groups of Europe, however, the Slavs appeared more resistant to foreign influence and their strange "adoption" of Christianity is arguably the most pagan in form, perhaps because the Slavic nations (with some exceptions for those in central Europe) were largely spared from the continent's religious wars, the Renaissance, Inquisitions, the Protestant Reformation, and the Enlightenment, all of which reshaped and redefined religious belief in Europe in various ways, but had the common effect of further severing Europeans from pagan religion and traditions as new ideology uprooted old ideology, leaving the past in obscurity.

Spared from such troubles (though there was the specter of Communism to contend with, later), the Slavic peoples largely retained a very pagan form of worship and tradition that suffered only a thin veneer of Christianity, allowing some ancient Slavic pagan traditions to survive to the modern day relatively unchanged. One example of an ancient Slavic tradition that survived to the modern day, with minimal foreign influence, is "Kupala Night," also known as

"Ivan Kupala," a Summer Solstice festival that is celebrated on two different evenings, depending on whether the original pagan or later Christian date is celebrated: the night between June 23rd and 24th or the night between July 6th and 7th, respectively. The holiday's earliest written mention is in the chronicles of Tver (now the Russian Federation) in 1175, though it is understood that the holiday had been celebrated for centuries beforehand.

"Kupala" (from the Proto-Slavic kupati, "to bathe") is a pagan Slavic goddess representing water, healing, love, the harvest, the removal of

evil spirits, and fire. Being a goddess of both fire and water may seem contradictory, but the common element linking the two is the idea of natural cleansing, which was one of the primary aspects of Kupala; the ability to rectify the impure and bring joy through health and the banishment of evil spirits. Kupala's traditional symbols are water, flowers, birch trees, ferns, and fire. The celebration of Kupala Night was not only a celebration of fertility and cleansing, but a celebration of the harmonious joining of opposite elements: water and fire, male and female, and moon and sun.

Per the original Pagan

"Rites of Belarusians" depicted on postage stamps issued by Belarus

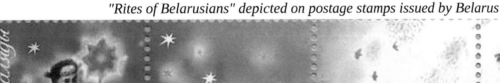

Botanical depiction of Osmunda regalis

lic L.   Königsfarn.

tradition, Kupala Night began on the evening of June 23rd, though during the day young and unmarried women busy themselves with the construction of garlands to wear on their heads. In the early evening, these women would go out into the forest and meadows to collect healing herbs and other plants such as purple loosestrife, euphorbia, rue, pansies, ferns, cornflowers, and others. As Kupala was the god of healing and purity, these plants were believed to be imbued with special powers on Kupala Night and would be collected for use in medicine as well as placed within the walls of homes to ward off evil spirits.

After the garland-adorned women would enter the forest in search of these plants, young men would follow them to assist in the search for medicinal herbs and flowers. Most sought after – and elusive – was the fern *Osmunda regalis*, known as the "flowering fern" or "Perun's flower" after Perun, the Slavic god of thunder, fire, and war. While ferns are not flowering plants, *Osmunda regalis* will produce goldish-red and fire-like fronds that appear similar to flowers, making the plant unique among ferns and traditionally imbued with otherworldly powers. Per legend, Perun's flower blooms only at midnight on Kupala Night and would bring long-lasting luck and prosperity to anyone who managed to find it, though the flower was jealously guarded by demons. To successfully pick the flower one must find the plant before midnight, draw a magic circle around it, and wait; movement outside of the circle before the fern flower was picked would cause the demons to attack. Once the fern blossoms and the flower are picked, the harvester was completely safe from demons due to the flower's magical properties and would be granted health, good luck, and the ability to speak to and understand trees and plants.

The young men and women scouring the woods for herbs would assist in the fostering of relationships, and if a man came out of the woods wearing the garland of one of the women, it symbolized that the couple had become engaged. After the search for magical herbs and flowers was over, the youth would gather at a nearby stream or river and engage in divination with the women's

6

garlands. The women would take off their garlands and set them afloat on the water to be carried away by the current. If the wreaths sank it was a sign that the woman was to have ill fortune in her love life; if the wreath sailed on, it was a sign of good luck regarding the same.

After the divination on the river, people gathered around a bonfire and ate a ceremonial dinner of eggs, *veraschaka* (a type of gravy made from sausages), *vareniki* (also known as pierogi; a type of dumpling filled with quark, meat, cabbage, or sometimes berries), and liquor. Celebrants would dance around the bonfire and sing songs, often with erotic tones, in celebration of fertility. Celebrants would also jump over the bonfire as a means of cleansing the soul, young couples often jumping together arm-in-arm. Additionally, clothing of the sick would be tossed in the fire, believing that the fire would also help rid disease, and celebrants would rid themselves of old herbs gathered on the previous Kupala Night, it being taboo to discard such healing herbs in a way other than by Kupala's fire. The last fire-related activity was the creation of the "Sun wheel," an oiled wheel (sometimes woven or adorned with dry straw) that was hoisted to the top of a pole to symbolize the sun. In some instances, the Sun wheel would be rolled down a hill until its fire smoldered out, symbolizing the waning powers of the Sun after the end of the summer solstice. In other regions, the Sun wheel would be replaced

with an effigy of Kupala, which would be lit on fire before being extinguished in water and strewn about in fields, again symbolizing the declining power of summer after the solstice.

At dawn, people would wash themselves with the dew collected during Kupala's night, and would run through dew-laden fields, believing that the dew would assist them in getting married faster. The sick would also roll in the dew-laden fields in attempts to rid themselves of disease.

Kupala Night remained one of the most popular holidays of the year, and despite

the official Slavic conversion to Christianity in 988 C.E., the holiday continued to be celebrated in its original form. Though Christian clergy viewed the celebration as perverse and attempted to ban its celebration, they quickly realized that old habits are hard to break, and the peasantry continued to celebrate their native pagan faith regardless of the clergy's demands. Unable to completely eradicate Kupala Night, the Christian clergy decided instead to support its celebration and "adopt" it into the Church, changing certain elements to shoehorn the celebration into the Christian pantheon. Kupala was replaced with the figure of

Night of Ivan Kupala by Klavdy Lebedev

Ivan Kupala ("Ivan" being the Slavic name for "John"), a figure modeled after John the Baptist. Water elements of Kupala Night were restyled as elements of baptism, still maintaining the original elements of purity and cleansing. Herbs gathered during the festival would also be blessed by priests, thereby imbuing them with special medicinal powers. Substantively, the holiday was exactly the same, the only difference being the movement of magical power from pagan figures and elements to Christian ones.

The Christian clergy's attempt to uproot the holiday was only partially successful, however, as a "dual faith" developed, creating two camps: one that celebrates the original pagan celebration between June 23rd and 24th (per the Julian calendar, a pre-Christian calendar) and another that celebrated the "Christian" version, sometimes on the night of July 6th and 7th if the Gregorian

Ivan Kupala on a Russian Stamp

calendar had been adopted (mostly in Catholic regions, as opposed to Orthodox). So prominent and obvious was the existence of paganism and Christianity that the Slavs developed names for the phenomenon, such as *dvaevyerie* in Russian– a transliteration of "двоеверие," which in itself is a hybrid of the Russian words for "two" (dva, два) and "faith" (dovyerie, доверие).

Having been spared from the bulk of the religious wars in Western Europe, the Slavs maintained this sense of "dual-faith" until the Bolshevik Revolution and the establishment of the Soviet Union, which began to stamp out any form of religious belief in favor of state atheism. Although the Soviet Union and other communist governments in Eastern Europe made religious traditions such as Kupala Night risky to celebrate, state atheism and the overarching Cold War strangely kept Slavic traditions and the sense of "dual faith" locked in time. As religious traditions such as Kupala Night arose in societies dominated by agriculture and a large peasant class, prior to the introduction of rapid industrialization, urbanization, and materialism, the cutting off of foreign influence on religious traditions meant that the concept of Kupala Night, both in its original pagan and its Christian form, hardly evolved beyond the format it had near the end of the First World War. After the fall of the Soviet Union and other communist satellite governments in Eastern Europe, the Slavic "dual faith" found itself restored and largely unchanged, notably lacking the strong materialist elements that had pervaded the traditions of Western Europe during the same century.

Of course, state atheism had largely eroded religious belief within the Slavic nations, particularly those of the former Soviet Union, and though the cultural effect of this "dual faith" is still visible in many Slavic countries, it is often sans "faith." Regardless, the widespread lack of sincere belief in the religious elements of Kupala Night, either pagan or Christian, has no effect on the communal benefits the holiday brings nor did the lack of religious belief prevent the holiday from regaining popularity after the fall of the Iron Curtain. If anything, the recent resurgence of

Kupala Night by Sokolov

nationalism within the Slavic countries (though the author disagrees, it can be argued that the communist nations of Europe always had a nationalistic character, but this argument is splitting definitional hairs) has contributed to the resurrection of old pagan traditions or their Christian knock-offs, primarily because of their communal elements and cultural importance.

Kupala Night continues to be celebrated today throughout Eastern Europe but, given its association with natural elements such as fields, rivers, and fire, the primary areas where the holiday is celebrated in its original form are in rural towns and villages, with larger cities hosting festivals that lack the natural and agrarian-based features of the holiday. Kupala Night remains popular (though it may be called by different names) in countries such as Poland, Lithuania, Latvia, Estonia, Ukraine, Belarus, and Russia, among others with strong Slavic history. Overall Kupala Night and the effects of Slavic "dual faith" are a prime example of the "strangeness" of the Slavs that so often perplexes the more Western European nations: while they are certainly European and have much in common with the modern West, Slavic isolation from foreign influence and the retention of an old-world sense of community and tradition sets them apart and remains a point of both intrigue and tension between the Slavic nations and other nations in Europe.

For further reading:

Phillips, Charles, and Michael Kerrigan. Forests of the Vampire: Slavic Myth. Edited by Tony Allan, Time-Life Books BV, Amsterdam, 1999.

Many good sources on Slavic paganism and mythology sadly remain unavailable in English. The author would, therefore, like to thank his friend, Darya, for assisting in the translation of information from Belarusian and from Russian where his own knowledge failed, and for giving personal insight on Kupala Night celebrations in Belarus. Спасибо большое за помощь!

Stribog enjoys traveling, learning more about his ancestral heritage, and learning about the traditions of European communities, particularly taking an interest in how history and other socio-geographical factors shape cultural identities and make them unique.

The Knowlton Henge Complex:

Where the Old Faith Meets the New

by Traditionalist

All photos provided by Traditionalist for this piece

I've always felt a deep connection to "place," a feeling that I can't really describe or explain and which, at times, seems almost mystical. Some might attribute this to the *anima locus,* or elemental spirits, or even to the gods; but however it's interpreted, I have always felt a deep affinity for the ancient, solitary and atmospheric landscapes of my homeland, the British Isles.

One place that stirs such feelings is Knowlton Henge near Wimborne in East Dorset, which I visited for the first time in 2015. Immediately it seemed the kind of liminal place that is

experienced and not just visited. I was there on an overcast afternoon when few others were about, apart from an occasional dog walker, which meant I had the place pretty much to myself.

Dominating the site are the ruins of a Norman church situated within a late Neolithic to early Bronze Age ring or circle. Clearly, the church represents an attempt to Christianize an ancient, pagan site, since its location in the center of the henge cannot possibly be fortuitous. I took the opportunity to walk around the perimeter of the circle before exploring the ruined church

itself.

The ancient earthwork comprises a circular embankment up to four meters high with an internal ditch almost 11 meters wide. The henge is somewhat oval in shape and more than 100 meters across at its widest point. There are two entrances, one at the northeast and one at the southwest, although it is unclear, as a result of subsequent modifications to the site, whether these represent original features.

In fact, this earthwork is only the central part of a larger ceremonial landscape located in the upper valley of the River

Allen. There are four other associated earthworks, two of which are also best described as henges: the D-shaped "Northern Henge" and the much larger "Southern Henge" (the latter now partly occupied by a farm and bisected by a road). Two other nearby circular earthworks are not so easily interpreted: the "Old Churchyard" and the tree-covered "Great Barrow." These may or may not be contemporaneous with the other henges.

However, it is the central circle, containing the church, to which most visitors are drawn. The church itself was built in the twelfth century and underwent modification in the fourteenth. But the village it served was ravaged by the Black Death and soon thereafter abandoned, though the church continued to be used until the eighteenth century, when its roof finally collapsed.

During my leisurely stroll around the circle, it wasn't until I reached the north-northeast side that I noticed it – a stand of yew trees just outside the circle, festooned with colorful ribbons, ornaments and notes. Yew trees, of course, have long-standing pagan associations, and recent scientific work has suggested that the Knowlton yews may well date back to the pre-Christian period. I discovered later that the locals call this "the wishing tree", and, as the wind gently swayed the yews' branches, the trees themselves seemed to whisper that the Old Faith, the old traditions, had not yet died out, nearly a thousand years since Christianity had imposed itself at the site.

Indeed, just as the colorfully-decorated yews hearken back to the original, ceremonial use of the site, to a time before the newcomers had arrived, so too do the folk tales, myths and legends associated with Knowlton. According to legend, there were several other, unsuccessful attempts to construct a church at the site before the present one. It is said that each night the partially constructed building would

disappear, almost as though the Christian takeover was being actively resisted by the pagan spirits of Knowlton.

Another local tale says that the bell ringers of nearby Sturminster Newton once stole the church bell, but, in order to evade their pursuers, disposed of it in White Mill Hole in the River Stour. By 1774 this story was already preserved in a local rhyme:

Knowlton bell is stole
And fallen into White Mill Hole.

But other accounts attribute the bell-stealing to the Devil, and record that he threw it into the River Allen, where attempts by the locals to retrieve it came to nothing. Folklorist Ralph Whitlock (p.102) points out that in such tales of conflict over sites, the Devil is a representation of the old gods, and, intriguingly, is usually seen to get his way!

Ghostly apparitions are also said to haunt Knowlton, including a spectral rider galloping on his horse across the henge as though the church is not there, presumably another echo of the site's pre-Christian past. A face is said to appear at the upper window of the church tower, though there is no longer a floor for anyone to stand upon, and a weeping lady, identified by some as a nun, has been seen kneeling outside the church. Visitors have also reported a tall black figure; most recently a lady with her two children who apparently saw the apparition pass before them in broad daylight.

The veil is undoubtedly thin at Knowlton Henge, whether we are speaking of the veil between paganism and Christianity, the past and the present, or this world and the next.

Bibliography and Further Reading:

Paul Adams, Eddie Brazil and Peter Underwood. Shadows in the Nave: A Guide to the Haunted Churches of England. Stroud: The History Press, 2011. (Knowlton Henge ghosts on pages 90-92.)

Robert Bevan-Jones. The Ancient Yew. Bollington: Windgather Press, 2002. (Knowlton Henge yews discussed on pages 103-106.)

John Gale. (2017). Knowlton Circles: A Later Neolithic and Early Bronze Age Ceremonial Complex and its Environs – A Review. Landscapes, Vol. 18, No. 2, pp. 102-119.

Allen Meredith and Janis Fry. (2016). Ageing the Yew. Quarterly Journal of Forestry, Vol. 110, No. 4, pp. 269-274.

Nigel Pennick. Anima Loci. Ogygia Series Number 4. Bar Hill: NIDECK, 1993.

Jennifer Westwood and Jacqueline Simpson. The Lore of the Land: A Guide to England's Legends, from Spring-Heeled Jack to the Witches of Warboys. London: Penguin Books, 2005. (Knowlton Henge folklore discussed on pages 215-216.)

Ralph Whitlock. In Search of Lost Gods: A Guide to British Folklore. London: Book Club Associates, 1979.

Traditionalist is an indigenous Briton with an enduring interest in the landscape, history, myths, legends and folklore of his home country. He can be found at **gab.ai/Traditionalist2**

RUNE ART
by Iwobrand

THE TIWAZ AETT

The Elder Futhark is traditionally separated into three groups of eight runes, the so-called *aetts*. In this issue of Mythic Dawn we feature ink drawings of the first aett, which is called **Tiwaz Aett**, because it is the aett starting with the Tiwaz rune in an *exoteric* reading of the runes.

The **Odal** rune however starts the esoteric reading of the runes. It represents the primordial and intricate origins, from which all form and number descend. To this day there is a law in Norway called the *Odelsrett*, which regulates the inheritance of family property. The Anglo-Saxon and German words for nobility seem to be related to this root as well: *Aethel* and *Adel*.

The second rune is the **Dagaz** rune, which represents the formation of a polarity, the two forces that forge any life, like hammer and anvil, sky and earth, the day ascending from the night.

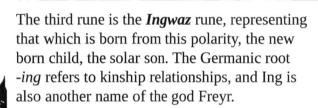

The third rune is the **Ingwaz** rune, representing that which is born from this polarity, the new born child, the solar son. The Germanic root *-ing* refers to kinship relationships, and Ing is also another name of the god Freyr.

The forth rune is the **Laguz** rune and cognate with the English word lake, representing the fertile forces of plant growth, water and the moon.

The fifth rune is called *Mannaz*, a cognate with the word man. Tacitus already mentions a mythic progenitor-figure called Mannus, from which all Germanic tribes descend, which is here reflected in the twosome nature of man. The rune also represents the correspondence of macrocosmos and microcosmos, man being an augmentation of the earth.

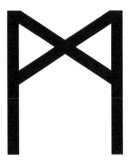

The sixth rune is called *Ehwaz* and means horse, an animal of high importance to Aryan culture. A horse pulls the sun in the *Trundholm* chariot. Other than runes, the Germanic people also used white horses for divination, which links the horse to the cosmic ride through space and time.

The seventh rune is called **Berkanan**, which is connected to the birch. The indigenous tree of the northern European flora is connected to female fertility due to its fair white bark. The word for birch was also a skaldic kenning for woman.

The eighth rune is called **Tiwaz**, linked to the god of the sky, war and justice, later known as Týr or Irmio, which is again linked to the Irminsul.

From the sources about runes that are passed down to us, we can conclude a certain basic meaning for every rune, conveyed in the text. The artistic interpretation of the runes however does mainly explore their pictogrammatic aspect, creating meaning by mere shape and form. Thereby comes about a wordless language on its own, which, just like divination and forecast, is linked to the recognition of patterns in natural order by the beholder.

Iwobrand is a German artist. You can follow him on Twitter at **@Iwobrand**.

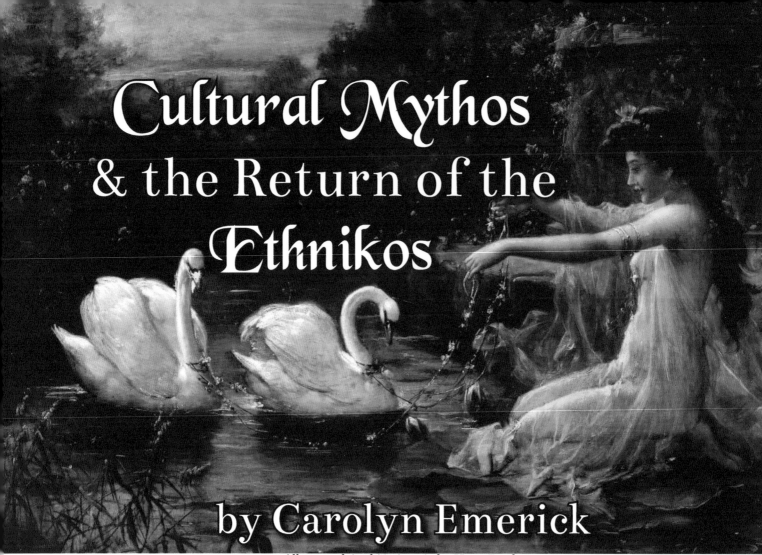

Cultural Mythos & the Return of the Ethnikos

by Carolyn Emerick

All artwork in this piece is by Hans Zatzka

That we live in an age devoid of cultural mythos has been observed by other notable thinkers in decades past. While the ramifications of this have been described and relayed to wide audiences, there is a disturbing lack of understanding of this among Westerners today. While many are awakening to the shock of gross cultural changes that are, in many ways, not to our benefit, too many lack insight into the role that the severance from our own indigenous ethnic mythos plays in social issues that we see at work today.

We have been told that mythology is the body of beliefs of primitive and barbaric people. And, we have been told that fairytales are simplistic tales told for children and simpletons (i.e. of value only for immature and underdeveloped minds). Moreover, the very words "myth" and "fairytale" are often used as synonyms to mean "falsehood" or even "lie." When a high-minded scientific rationalist uses the phrase "that's just a myth," where what he really means is "a fallacy," what does this do to the status of mythology in the subconscious conception of the general public? We can see by this example that it is not only the Abrahamic acculturation and destruction of the indigenous worldview of Europeans (and, subsequently, other ethnic groups worldwide) that has diminished the status of mythos in the minds of the Folk, but modern scientific rationalism is just as guilty. For, both of these worldviews are inherently dogmatic. Both foster a lofty frame of mind which peers down from its self-appointed pedestal to view the beliefs which came before as primitive, barbaric, and less than. Because mythos has been drastically reduced in status in the minds of Westerners in recent decades and centuries, it behooves us to consider just why it is that myth ever was important in the first place.

A Holistic Folk Culture

Anyone who begins to study mythology is quickly introduced to the field of linguistics. This is because most (though, not all) of the mythological pantheons in the European lexicon fall in the Indo-European mytho-linguistic family. What we find is that the mythological canons correlate alongside language families, thereby leading to comparative linguistic analysis. In other words, Hellenic (Greek) mythology is found among Greek language speakers, Roman myth is found among Latin speakers, Teutonic (Germanic/Norse) myth is found among Germanic language speakers, and so on. This relationship between myth and language is found universally worldwide, however the examples given here are from the Indo-European family, specifically. What this indicates is that language and mythos evolved side by side during the earliest gestations of what would become the human ethno-cultural groups we recognize today.

Scientific rationalists as well as Abrahamists are both quick to dismiss theories on the mythical worldview of Europeans from its earliest origins as well as its survival into more recent times. People "of the book" and people studied in "the scientific method" are both trained to require a point of reference that cannot be argued with. In other words, the science is proven by mathematical equation or is otherwise testable, whereas Abrahamists simply point to the books that they believe are the words of their god as indisputable fact. But, history, anthropology, psychology, and mythology (which bleeds into all of those fields) are interpretive in nature. We make our best assertion about what happened in the past based on a variety of evidence at hand. It has been asserted by many specialists who have devoted their lives to studying the mythology and/or the development of mankind that humans appear to have had some level of mythological worldview at the earliest stages of human development. Cave paintings, carved figurines, and burial arrangements have all suggested a level of shamanism with belief in the afterlife as early as the Paleolithic period, up to 30,000 years ago.

What this means is that the onset of Abrahamic universalism is only a tiny, tiny fraction of the overall human experience - the vast majority of which was rooted in animistic polytheism. However, not only was animistic polytheism the de facto worldview among virtually all human beings, it was quite specifically an ethnic-centric belief system. While universalist religions attempt to homogenize world cultures by absorbing heterogeneous people into their uni-myth, the irony is that polytheism was, indeed, universal. The big difference is that polytheism was ethnic-specific whereas universalism works to sever a culture from its indigenous ethnos. Polytheism and the pantheons of gods that it housed were rooted firmly in the very origins of the development of the cultures in which they lived. There were never names for these religions because they were simply the beliefs and gods of your own people. It was not until the advent of "revealed religion" (supposedly given by the supreme god to a prophet) that ethnic faith practitioners began to be referred to by derogatory terms like "pagan" and "infidel." In fact, in the original Greek version of the New Testament, the letters of Paul use the word "ethnikos" to refer to pagans. In other words, it was clear that these universalists had an intention of breaking people from their unique and diverse ethnic faiths to homogenize them into their universalist uni-faith.

What we see is that in the vast experience of humanity, human culture was one holistic whole; a whole which has been fractured ever more in recent eras of history. However, that first blow, at least in terms of European culture, was dealt squarely by the hands of Christianity. Whereas for thousands of years in cultural development, Slavic faith rooted in the Slavic mythological pantheon was synonymous with Slavic language and Slavic ethnos, suddenly one day Slavs were told that this Hebrew/Greek book was their

holy scripture. Whereas the land that nurtured generations of ethnic Slavs had been considered sacred for thousands of years, suddenly Slavs were told to place their eyes on Israel as their holy land and to look to the mytho-history of a completely unrelated people on another continent as the stories they should tell their children instead of the great deeds of their own tribal ancestors. Of course, I am using Slavs as an example of a cohesive European mytho-linguistic group, but this pattern unfolded clear across the European continent. Prior to this ethno-cultural assault, Slavs, Celts, Germans, Balts, Hellenes, and the other ethnic groups indigenous to Europe can be said to have been examples of Folk groups in a true, holistic sense.

What is Mythos?

We can see that mythos and ethnos had always gone hand in hand as part of one holistic *whole* state of being before universalist ideology began actively working to sever the "ethnikos" from their Folk identity. But what is ethnic mythos and why does this matter? As mentioned, all people of the world, when left in their indigenous, native state, held an animistic polytheist worldview. That definition should be expanded, however, to include ancestor veneration. The reverence of ancestors is, arguably, the very earliest form of religion and it goes hand in hand with animism. In an animistic worldview, it is believed that spirits dwell all around us in nature. Indeed, we viewed ourselves as *within* the natural paradigm instead of above it or outside of it. Animists believe that not only do animals have a spirit, but elements have spirits, spirits may dwell within inanimate objects, and even naturally occurring phenomena have a spirit attached to it. Therefore, within this worldview, when our loved ones pass from physical life, their spirit continues to dwell among us and can intercede in our lives.

This was a very tribalist worldview. It does seem to have been fairly universal worldwide, however this kind of worldview allows for ethnic variation. Mythos evolves alongside language, culture emerges within a specific landscape, and the tribe is very aware of the presence of their ancestors. This means that although this system was universal, it was not *universalist* or uniform.

Beliefs about spirits were tailored to the climate and landscape a tribal group lived within. Therefore, mythological systems developed that were unique to diverse ethnic groups existing worldwide. These mythological systems included deities, nature spirits, stories built up around these beings, superstitions and rituals pertaining to these entities and the tribal ancestors. In addition, rituals rooted in this holistic worldview also allowed for cultural transmission of codes of acceptable behavior as well as recognition of the passage of life stages.

As we can see, spiritual worldview was embedded in the very fibers of the concept of self. Identity was a fabric made up of many interwoven threads. Notion of one's self in relationship to his or her family, clan, and wider tribe was also placed in context of the land itself with the omnipresence of one's ancestors always guiding them. Of course, great chieftains and other important persons valued by the tribe may be remembered as *tribal* ancestors honored by everyone. So, mythos was not only simplistic stories told to children, but it was an entire worldview that was interlaced with language, ancestry, tribe, and geographic location.

Storytelling as Cultural Memory

Like ethnic mythos, storytelling can be said to be a universal human pastime. It was a way to share cultural ideals and morals, but also remember great deeds of important persons and place the tribe in context with those who came before them. We know that oral transmission was a favored method of cultural remembrance among Europeans and other ethnic groups. We know that storytellers and those in priest castes could devote decades to memorization of sacred lore. Stories such as the Anglo-Saxon epic poem, Beowulf, continued to be told to new generations of the tribes who would become known as the English to remind them of their origins in Scandinavia and their cultural identity as Teutonic people. In this same way, my own family and many other American families tell their children stories of our family ancestors and how they came to this country. These stories give individuals an understanding of their origins and a sense of identity. Arguably, people who do not grow up with some of kind of cultural grounding often express a feeling of rootlessness.

Because these stories

that were imbedded with imagery from our mythos, which was itself intertwined with our ethnos, developed over thousands of years and only evolved very slowly as we, ourselves, evolved culturally, stories that became widespread and deeply spiritual took on a mythic nature. A myth, rather than a simple story, carries with it gravitas and weight for how it has permeated the wider language family and holds deep meaning. The meaning could be a foundational spiritual understanding, such as cosmology and earth origins, or it could be the exploits of a deity who is especially powerful in the wider consciousness of the tribe. With this understood, the modern trend to use the term "myth" to mean "fallacy" is especially egregious. It is almost as if there is some agenda at work to twist our conception to believe that which was always deeply important to us as ethno-cultural groups should be disparaged and dismissed today.

Deeper Understandings from Great Teachers

To better understand the value that mythos holds for us, it can be helpful to look toward some of the great teachers of the last century who have already transmitted this important insight which has, seemingly, been forgotten (at least by mainstream society) all too soon. Arguably, the figure who has had the most impactful contribution to understanding the relationship between mythos and consciousness is Carl Jung.

While he looked at mythology through the lens of psychology, it is remarkable that he looked at mythology at all when one considers the sterile outlook of his field which leans toward scientific rationalism today. Jung wrote less on mythology in its own right, and more on how mythological elements existed in and affected the human consciousness. His work was, actually, heavily rooted in psychoanalysis with less time spent on analysis of myth, but he was the first influential figure to acknowledge the important role that myth plays in the consciousness of both the individual and the wider culture.

Jung was among the first to recognize the role that the archetype plays in the cultural psyche. In his "Archetypes and the Collective Unconscious" he says, "Another well known expression of the archetype is myth and fairytale. But here too we are dealing with forms that have received a specific stamp and have been handed down through long periods of time." He continues, "What the word 'archetype' means in the nominal sense is clear enough, then, from its relations with myth, esoteric teaching, and fairytale," (p5). He goes on to explain that how this relates to psychoanalysis is more complex, but we are mainly concerned with the main point: that mythic archetypes are a "stamp" or imprint that were formed and transmitted over vast stages of human existence.

Rather than criticizing

his own field (which was arguably in its earliest stages at the time he entered it and, therefore, there was not a vast body of work *to* criticize), Jung casts judgement on previous mythologists who observed the relationship between myth and natural and celestial happenings but failed to recognize the interplay between myth and our own human psyche. He says, "so far, mythologists have always helped themselves out with solar, lunar, meteorological, vegetal, and other ideas of the kind. The fact that myths are first and foremost a psychic phenomenon that reveal the nature of the soul is something they have absolutely refused to see until now," (p6). Well, of course, Jung was right to judge previous mythologists so harshly. However, most mythologists working prior to Jung were heavily biased with an Abrahamist lens which would, of course, prohibit them from seeing the important role that indigenous ethnic mythos does, indeed, play in the human psyche. Jung expounds on how mythos is impactful on both the ethnological level *and* upon the individual psyche.

Without Carl Jung's work to build upon, the most important mythologist of the 20th century very likely would not have burst onto the scene. I am, of course, speaking of Joseph Campbell. Like Jung, Campbell receives a fair amount of disdain from modern "scholars" in his field. But, again like Jung, this has not diminished his public appeal and the impact that his work has had upon thousands of readers. If Jung lamented the oversight of previous mythologists to recognize the importance of myth to the psyche, well, Campbell really went all the way for it. He studied, traveled, observed, and wrote extensively on the role of myth in worldwide cultures. In 1988, his lifetime of study was shared in the living rooms of thousands when Campbell joined Bill Moyers for a multipart series called "The Power of Myth," the transcript of which was later released in book form. In it, Campbell discusses the meaning of myth to societies and the repercussions that the lack of myth, as well as mythic rites and rituals, are in modern society.

Eerily, many of the societal problems that Campbell recognizes as a direct result of our lack of cultural mythos in the 1980s are even more prevalent in our world today, thirty years later. Campbell notes that our lack of myth-based rites of passage have rendered young people without guideposts for living and, thus, they often do not know how to behave properly – that is, with respect toward the cultural norms of the society in which they are living. In the discussion, Bill Moyers asks if this is not related to the American Evangelical calls to return to "old time religion," meaning Christianism. Campbell retorts that these calls are a "terrible mistake" because that form of religion is only

"vestigial" and it "doesn't serve life," (p15). This stood out prominently to me because now, 30 years on, we still have certain alternative right wing figures declaring that the downfall of Western society is due to our walking away from Judeo-Christian religion. Like Campbell, I call this a terrible mistake. I would assert that the downfall of Western society has more to do with the Abrahamic assault upon European ethnic mythos than any other factor. But, Campbell goes on to explain that the Biblical worldview was designed for a time and place so far removed

from Westerners today that it cannot work for our needs because it simply does not fit us, (p39-40). Of course, the lengthy discussion has much to say on the importance of myth and how to find personal myth in the modern world.

There is much more that could be said, but it would be remiss not to make room to mention the much beloved scholar and author, J.R.R. Tolkien. Of course, anyone who has read his fantasy novels or seen the films they inspired understands the important role that mythology played in his inspiration. But, there is a

lengthy essay based on a lecture that he once gave that delves into the realm of fairytale, called "On Fairy Stories." In it, Tolkien actually disagrees with something that Campbell says in "The Power Myth." Campbell insisted that fairytales were sort of like mini-myths for children, specifically designed to aid in crossing the threshold to adulthood. As someone who has spent some time studying them, I am more inclined to agree with Tolkien when he gave his lecture nearly 50 years prior to Campbell's talk and insisted that fairy stories were, essentially, a *human* interest, and therefore only of interest to children because children are small humans.

Circling back to the beginning, Tolkien also points out that our definitions are sorely lacking when we look to the dictionary to define "fairy story." Well, he says, that term is missing all together, so we must look to "fairytale." Tolkien also laments the negative definitions that he found in the dictionary to describe a fairytale as something that is not true. So he goes on to define it, although a definition is difficult to pin down. Tolkien explains that the realm of "Faerie" is actually a state of being. It encompasses all manner of the supernatural, as well as the natural world, in addition to mortal humans – when we are enchanted. He describes the fairy story as a "soup" that originates in history that has been simmered with imagination.

This, I think, is where myth and fairytale meet with Jung's theories about their role in our psyches. These tales cannot be separated from history because they originate there and live through time within history – yet also outside of it. They are outside history inasmuch as they live in the imagination. Yet, these stories are not separate from history, though we do not categorize them as history.

There are, of course, many more points and tidbits upon which could be elaborated. However, the main point that bears emphasis is that mythos is part of the human experience. It is not only what makes us human, but it is part of what makes us unique and diverse ethnic groups in the world. The agenda working to grind us all up through a meat grinder and obscure our unique characteristics as it

churns us out as homogenized human sausages has been at work since Saul of Tarsus adopted the name of Paul and set out with a mission to evangelize the "ethnikos" within the Roman Empire. But, with corporate elites putting political pressure to increase globalization for materialist reasons today, the threat to unique diversity in the world is ever more real.

And, yet, it is in this environment that more and more "ethnikos" are eschewing the Abrahamic and overly rationalist dogmas and looking for our deeper cultural connections. Although this discussion painted quite a bleak picture while outlining the attacks our ethnic mythos has faced over the centuries, the good news is that threads of it did survive over the ages. Revival and interest in cultural mythology is booming throughout the West as we speak. Digging in deep and doubling down on our "ethnikos" identity may be *the* very best way we can preserve our ethnic diversity and fight back against those who seek to destroy it.

Bibliography & Further Reading:

Campbell, Joseph. Primitive Mythology. New York: Arkana, 1991. print.

—. The Power of Myth. New York: Anchor Books, 1988.

Hartland, Edwin Sidney. The Science of Fairy Tales; An Inquiry into Fairy Mythology. London: Walter Scott, 1891.

Jung, Carl. Archetypes and the Collective Unconscious. New York: Princeton University Press, 1969.

—. Wotan. Zurich: Fretz & Wasmuth, 1936.

Leeming, David. From Olympus to Camelot: The World of European Mythology. New York: Oxford University Press, 2003. Print.

Tolkien, J.R.R. On Fairy Stories. 1939.
<http://brainstorm-services.com/wcu-2004/fairystories-tolkien.pdf>.

Carolyn Emerick is the editor of Mythic Dawn and Europa Sun magazines. She has a bachelor's degree in literature, graduate level training in archival studies, and has been studying European cultural heritage for most of her life. See her work at **CarolynEmerick.com**.

by Renwylf

Crafting a Heritage

A young woodcrafter, by Wilhelm Marc, 1895

The sun is high and hot as I stand against the stone wall at the edge of the narrow street in front of my house, avoiding the gaze of the locals passing by on foot. My concentration is already divided between my own task at hand and the one my son is undertaking beside me. We are woodworking; crafting sigils with rasp and chisel, objects that reflect the deepest places of our souls.

On a long flight across the Pacific, the inspiration to begin crafting with my children with the purpose of passing on European heritage began to manifest. I had just spent a vacation visiting family in America and was returning to my home in Japan. Having just visited the place of my birth, it was heavy on my heart that my life in Japan was so far removed from my own native culture, and I knew there were important ideas I wanted my children to inherit, concepts that went beyond pop-music and video games. Somewhere below the surface, an unvoiced question stirred: how does a father pass culture to the next generation in this modern world?

During the course of a nine-hour flight, two complimentary videos came together and planted seeds in my mind. The first was a documentary on skilled crafters who created works of art representative of their indigenous culture, and the second was an episode from season 3 of the T.V. series "Vikings," in which the character Floki is sculpting in his own sacred place, carving longship figureheads from large blocks of wood. The representations of Viking gods were so captivating to behold that I felt compelled to begin my own work, not just for myself but for my children.

Shipbuilding fascinated me from an early age, but it wasn't just any ship that grabbed my interest. When I was a teenager, I declared that before I die, I wanted to build a Viking longboat. In my youth, I lacked the skills and materials to undertake such a colossal feat, but I did content myself making wooden swords and other weapons in my father's garage. Now, I'm grateful that my children have taken to the woodworking trade with equal enthusiasm.

As a former Christian, I was well aware of the purported dangers of graven images. To create a representation of Yahweh was idolatry, yet all my Christian friends idolized singers, performers, and had no qualms about wearing symbols on t-shirts or putting posters on their walls. In the absence of meaningful symbols from the earth, natural archetypes that orient the psyche, perpetuate gratitude, and anchor us to our environment, we have been sold false symbols that serve consumerism and the will of the power elite.

The blessing of working with our hands is a time-honored tradition passed down from antiquity. Contrasting with the pace of modern life, crafting forces us to slow down and experience the process of creation with our bodies, physically manifesting symbols like the Mjolnir sigil I am currently polishing. Symbols of strength

A Merry Moment, Rzhevskaya Antonina, 1897

are in short supply in this age, surely by design of those who would keep us docile and cowed. But I want my children to know the strength of Thor.

In contrast to the Yahweh of my youth, the Father God I am seeking to know is Odin through images. I have only begun to understand the All-Father. He may be known by his face, by his missing eye given for wisdom. And Odin is distinct with his hat and spear. Perhaps even more than that, he may be known by the company he keeps. Though he is father of the gods, his companions are ravens and wolves and mighty Sleipnir.

It is my desire to pass on more to my children than my father passed to me. Perhaps this calling is part of the zeitgeist of this age, a response to growing polarization in the absence of true culture. Even if crafting is but a shadow of past, just a taste of the intense reality of living daily with the looming specter of death, it is a good step towards knowing our ancestors. Whether or not future generations will seek after such rewards remains to be seen, but it is certainly our calling to start pointing the way.

Renwylf writes on topics of interest including spirituality and Norse Shamanism.

Norwegian flag and VIking longship by WikiMedia user Jack_IOM

The Young Mechanic, by Allen Smith Jr., 1848

The Bardic Hearth

First to Rise

by Eric the Read

Fires rage all around,
searing hands that grasp for more.
A furious beast wild on the land,
a tide that billows with a ruinous roar.

Dawn now breaks within the wood,
where only blackened ghosts remain.
Softest Ash has replaced the living litter,
where the hardy saplings had grown in vain.

Who shall be first to claim such broken ground?
For a fertile land, many suitors abound.
What of the fruitful Beech? The blood-berried Rowan?
Will the lanky Willow soon be growin'?

Then from the earth cold and untilled
stirs the promise of life at last fulfilled.
For up from the ash cold and white,
springs forth the Berkano Bride tall and bright.

Slender as the Willow wand,
pale as the clouds so fair.
When she and her kin grow around the pond,
their golden manes brighten the Autumn air.

In time, more shall rise, too.
From the solid Oak to the knotted Yew.
When shall the wood be whole?
None can surmise.
But it all began with the first to rise.

Eric the Read is a gardener, an aspiring writer, a proud Asatrur, and above all a red-blooded American male who endeavors to remain free in the turbulent culture of the Wolf Age. When not pondering history or the written word, he is sometimes seen out of doors wandering the wilds.

Image by Eugene Kruger

Hail Victory!
by Traditionalist

Marching feet, an army roused
A battle to be won
The rising of the radiant wheel
Behold, Europa Sun!

Marching feet, an army roused
A drumbeat meant to warn
The rising of the Sonnenrad
Behold, the Mythic Dawn!

Traditionalist is an indigenous Briton with an enduring interest in the landscape, history, myths, legends and folklore of his home country. He can be found at **gab.ai/Traditionalist2**

Image by Maximilian Pirner

The Fates by by Elihu Vedder, 1887

Nine Lines Spun by the Norns

by
Juleigh Howard-Hobson

Storms never last, winter abates,
Though endtimes come, new dawn awaits.
The gods will help but every man
Weaves his own wyrd with his own hand.
Read runes, scan skies, but do not bless
The ice until it's crossed. Success
Depends on wisdom, nothing less
Than how and why you understand
This: Orlog fastens men to fates.

Julieigh Howard-Hobson is an accomplished writer. Please see "We Are The Maidens" for her full bio.

Freyja and the Necklace,
James Doyle Penrose

Met by Freya

A Poem in Homophone Chain Verse

by Ash Donaldson

For long I wandered a desolate road,
rode after strange creeds and faker isms.
Chrisms also I took, a holy wafer,
a way for me to know magic was real.

Firm knowledge, not belief, I sought,
saw it in others' eyes, or so it would seem,
seamless joining of men and God
gotten from who knows where.

I studied the books, kneeled in prayer rapt,
wrapped in bravado, my doubts to hide,
hied away from heresies, my days I wiled,
wild images of God's judgment before me.

Convinced of right, I hairsplit the sects.
Sex, however, I could not bridle,
bridal thoughts to Jesus praying,
preying upon my troubled mind.

Then one late summer, walking in a daze,
days flitting by without any solace,
soulless I felt, aimless, a knight with no sword,
sore despite the serenity about me.

Down from Christian shrine I tracked,
tracts in my hand, holding beads like a vise,
vice and virtue warring for a mind without sense,
scents and sights unnoticed around me.

Then a shrill cry broke my trance, as a raven cawed;
caught in branches, his wings fluttered and whirred.
Wordless he was but not speechless, feathers worn,
warning me not to sleep through life, so brief.

With eyes newly opened I looked across the vale,
veiled in lush flora and deepening mist,
missed while I'd sought concord with Rome,
roaming through a fallen, flawed world.

It was then that I shook off the Cross and its weight
waiting no more for a perfect God to judge my soul.
Solely my own, its wrongs and its worth, its growth or rot
Wrought by me, not Devil-tempted or God-compelled.

And then, through gathering storm-clouds of rain,
reining her cats, she came, chariot thunder-wheeled,
wielding beauty, her eyes blue as the ocean-tide,
tied up in braids, her long flaxen hair.

Intruding on long years of maudlin worship
warship now appeared, with no mast or
master, only mistress, Goddess Beautiful in Tears,
tiers of hair framing a face beyond words.

Enchantress and mother, she is no maid
made of shyness, no cloistered nun.
None but lovers may her aid broach,
brooch of Brisingamen above her breasts.

Yet for this, sullen monks called her vile,
vials of fragrance they smashed, burned the verses,
versus Vanadís they fought, but in vain.
Veins ice-cold, they fought quickening Desire.

With all comers, they said, she'd whored,
hordes of suitors seeking lustful acts.
Axe in one hand, in the other a rood,
rudely they tore down what none of them could build.

To the sheep-like Christian I paid no heed.
He'd try his grip on desire to tighten –
Titan or dwarf, though, he'd find himself thrown,
throne-perched Freya smiling all the while.

The same insults were better crafted by Loki;
low-key they sound in this latter hour.
Our age finds the free flow of poetry dammed –
damned, that is, for the demon-haunted.

Not as the Christian prays,
praise I Valfreya the holy.
Wholly hers am I, yet unbowed.
"Bow down" is a thing she'll never say.

In her sacred hall, there is no trace of guilt.
Gilt of honey-flowers welcomes hers to that isle.
I'll dine with her in Sessrúmnir ere
heir of mine toasts at the funeral feast.

Do not, then, think me odd,
awed by her presence,
presents I give, gifts of rhymes on
rime's onset, the chill days of autumn.

Ash Donaldson is a veteran of the Iraq War and holds a Ph.D. (ABD) in history. His work has been published in Counter-Currents and Europa Sun. A refugee from academia, he lives in exile somewhere in the Midwest.

Freyja by John Bauer

Artwork by Galileo Chini

Celestial Blessings
by Carolyn Emerick

'O Vakarine, daughter of the night,
harness the past to set things right.
Bind that which has inflicted harm,
to ready me for thy sister's warmth.

For, hark! I hear the sound of horns
that herald the Lady of the Morn!
Her arrival signals the end of strife.
Ausrine, the Bringer of New Life.

And, when little saplings begin to grow,
have faith and hope, for inside we know
that Saule, the Sun, Mother of all
is sending her blessings. To us they befall.

Carolyn Emerick writes about European history
and folk belief. Her poetry is collected in Pagan
Poems Vols I & II. **CarolynEmerick.com**

Source of it All
by Jared George

The swirl of the world,
the dance of the game.
On the tips of our tongues,
the spells that will change.

The cage 'round our minds
and the drain on our hearts.
Our histories now changed,
our parts we've forgot.

To come through this turn,
to rise from this fall.
Must we draw once again,
from the source of it all.

Jared George operates **The Great Order** website
and **YouTube** channel to help rehabilitate health,
meaning, and virtue in the ravaged West. Please
visit **TheGreatOrder.com** for more.

Artwork by Walter Crane

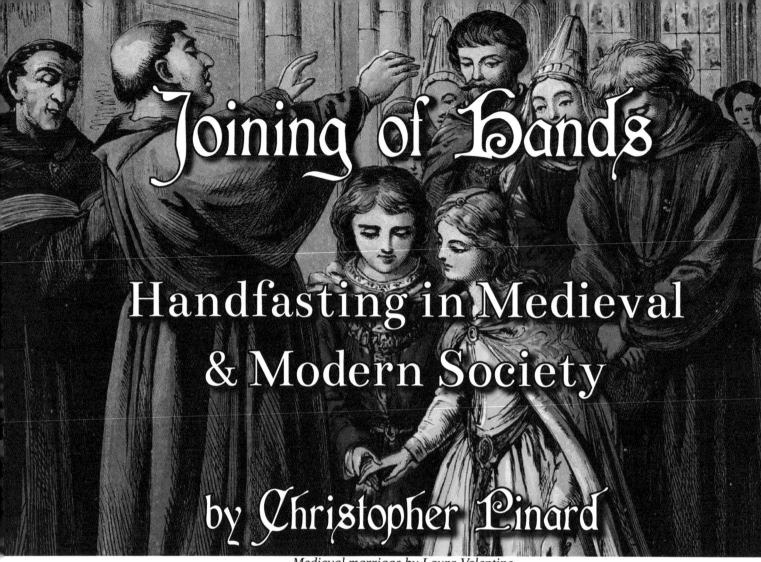

Joining of Hands

Handfasting in Medieval & Modern Society

by Christopher Linard

Medieval marriage by Laura Valentine

Revival of Handfasting

The popularity of handfasting among pagans owes a debt of gratitude to Gerald Gardner. Handfasting was an archaic word that had long fallen into disuse, only occasionally found in publications from folklore societies or in medieval studies classes. In 1951 when the Witchcraft Act of 1735 was repealed, occultists and Neo-pagans had the legal authority to conduct ceremonies in their own fashion. This led Gardner, as well as others, to seek out antiquarian terms to use instead of the word "wedding," which happened to have Christian connotations.

Eventually, Gardner and his entourage settled on the word handfasting. Since then, much romanticism has arisen surrounding the origin of the word. Many claim that handfasting was an ancient Celtic custom, but is that truly the case?

Gardner originally stated that he had been initiated into a coven in the New Forest area, and while he wasn't able to divulge the secrets imparted to him, he was quick to establish a religion based on the principles that he learned. Historians have found many holes in Gardner's claims. However, whether Gardner truly encountered this

coven or not, he undoubtedly founded one of the 20th centuries more vibrant religions. The early years of Wicca's founding saw adherents claiming a Celtic ancestry for the religion, including the origins of the handfasting concept. However, was this claim based on fact, romanticism, or something else?

Impact of WWII

During and after WWII, England saw a resurgence in interest in all things Celtic. Minimizing their own Anglo-Saxon (Germanic) roots allowed the English to see Germany solely as an enemy, rather than being cultural cousins. Wicca was just one of the many movements that chose to overinflate their Celtic ties during this period. Having already been a stigmatized community, it made no sense to further exacerbate the issue by declaring Germanic origins for the religion. Hence, handfasting began to be associated with Celtic culture as opposed to Germanic.

Etymology of Handfasting

The etymology of the word handfasting is relatively easy to trace. Similar words exist within other Germanic languages. Within Danish one finds the word *Håndfæstning* , in Norwegian one finds *Håndfestning* or *Handfesta*, meaning "to strike a bargain by joining hands" The associated customs were commonplace within these areas from the 12th to 17th Century. Looking to Norway, Sweden, and Denmark, the word håndfæsting was associated with legalities. Specifically, the word denoted circumstances and documents that involved oath taking. Denmark and Sweden both created documents similar to the Magna Carta, which were denoted as "håndfæstning." Essentially this oath required that the king be a just ruler. Further, it helped to delineate who the king would appoint to certain positions, as well as ensure that time-honored customs and traditions would be upheld. Being that marriage is not only a religious custom, but also a civil one, it is easy to see how such matters would also fall under the title of "handfasting." Further, the oath taking within a marriage

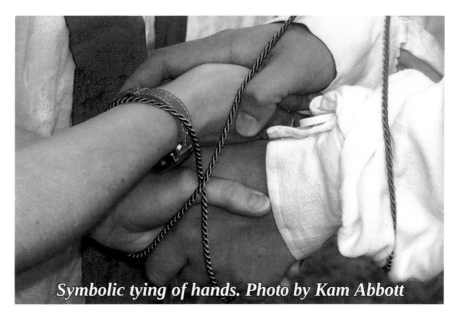

Symbolic tying of hands. Photo by Kam Abbott

ceremony parallel this legal custom.

Reassessing Handfasting's Origins

While it might be disappointing to many Neopagans, handfasting is recorded most notably as a Christian custom from the medieval period. This is understandable, due to the fact that this timeframe was denoted by the power that the Church wielded over society. Thus, those recordings that are preserved of the custom are Christian in nature because people of the period were, in fact, Christian. While many websites attribute the custom to "Pagan" Celts, there simply is no evidentiary support for that assertion. Rather, there is considerably more support for a Germanic origin.

So, if the word itself is tied to people of Teutonic culture, is it possible that this word was grafted onto a pre-existing custom at a later date? To determine this, it

would be imperative to assess what characteristics handfasting exhibits, most notably the handbinding with a cord, and the year and a day trial period.

The Isle of Man

In the 1600s Gaelic Scholar Martin Martin noted that "It was an ancient custom in the Isles that a man take a maid as his wife and keep her for the space of a year without marrying her; and if she pleased him all the while, he married her at the end of the year and legitimatized her children; but if he did not love her, he returned her to her parents." What is less clear is exactly how ancient this custom was. Simply, was the tradition created before or after the Viking settlement of the Isle of Man in the 800 and 900s? This cannot be clearly determined. It is notable that within the book "Women In Old Norse Society," Jenny Jochens writes that it wasn't uncommon for Vikings to have a long engagement period, sometimes extending from one to three years due to their transitory nature (pinning down a date that allowed for all family to be present was troublesome). Therefore, a year-long betrothal might seem pragmatic in such conditions. Prior to this mentioning by Martin, no quotes can be located which specify that handfasting was of a year timeframe, quite the opposite. Medieval English records denote that a handfasting was a betrothal to be married (an engagement), and that a marriage in the Church was required for religious reasons. However, it should be noted that these handfastings were in fact legally durable. In effect, they were an early form of civil union. Such unions could only be terminated by death, seeing that divorce was not a possibility yet. So, the idea that handfasting could be terminated after a year would not fit in line with what is known of the period.

Brehon Law

In order to try to determine if there is any possible connection to the pagan Celts with respects to this marriage custom, it would be of benefit to look at the many types of marriage that could exist under Brehon Law. In the Cáin Lánamna one can locate ten types of union: "(1) union of common contribution; (2) union of a woman on a man's contribution; (3) union of a man on a woman's contribution with service; (4) union of a woman who accepts a man's solicitation; (5) union of a man who visits the woman, without work, without solicitation, without provision, without material contribution; (6) union by abduction; (7) union of wandering mercenaries; (8) union by criminal seduction; (9) union by rape; (10) union of mockery." Nowhere within this document is a marriage of a single year or trial marriage mentioned.

Handbinding and Oath-Taking

The other most notable characteristic of modern handfastings is the hand binding with rope or ribbon. When researching medieval handfastings not a single reference was made to tying of the hands together. This appears to be a strictly modern invention. Likely this was an addition made by Gardner or other individuals in the post Victorian era, simply based on the notion that handfasting involves bringing two hands together. But rather than binding them with rope, the custom of handshaking of a sorts was inferred.

So then, if handfasting can't be tied to ancient Celtic customs, then is it strictly a medieval invention? Not exactly, it indeed has older origins. As indicated with the Germanic origin of the word, the tradition originates with the Teutonic people. Historians are very familiar with the fact that among the greater Germanic people (English, German, Danish, Swedish, Norwegian, Icelandic, Dutch, etc.), oath taking was a custom of vital importance. Before these modern nation states existed, Germanic peoples were part of a language and cultural family that spanned through most of Northwest Europe. Therefore it stands to reason that the later nation states would share cultural norms. This is evidenced with the

Medieval wedding, by Edmund Blair Leighton

prominence of oath taking throughout northwest Europe. In the Viking age, oath taking rings are a noted part of Norse culture. However they undoubtedly have older origins. In the late Classical period Tacitus noted that the Chatti carried rings of iron. It is highly probable that these rings were also oath-taking rings.

Troth and Anglo-Saxons

Among the Viking age peoples, marriage involved a similar oath taking ritual. It is likely that due to the oath taking nature of the marriage ceremony, it became associated with the word handfasting. The English custom involved taking one another by the hand and pledging troth to each other. Such a pledge might take the form of the following "I (Groom) take thee (Bride) to my wedded husband/wife, till death us depart, and thereto I plight thee my troth." Due to this exchange, the custom also went by the name of Troth Plight. Troth is also a word of Germanic origin, hinting once again to a Teutonic origin for the custom. Troth essentially translates to faithfulness, truth, or honesty. This is similar to arguments made by A. Anton in his work Handfasting in Scotland "Among the people who came to inhabit Northumbria and the Lothians, as well as among other Germanic peoples, the nuptials were completed in two distinct phases. There was first the betrothal ceremony and later the giving-away of the wife to the husband. The betrothal ceremony was called the beweddung in Anglo-Saxon because in it the

future husband gave weds or sureties to the woman's relatives, initially for payment to them of a suitable price for his bride but later for payment to her of suitable dower and morning-gift. The parties plighted their troth and the contract was sealed, like any other contract, by a hand-shake. This joining of hands was called a handfæstung in Anglo-Saxon."

Scotland and Handfastings

Looking once again to Scotland, it appears that in the 18th and 19th centuries there were two notable references made on handfasting. Thomas Pennant in his "Tour of Scotland," and Sir Walter Scott in his novel, "The Monastery," both mention handfasting as being a trial form of marriage. A. Anton, in "Handfasting in Scotland," wrote that Pennant and Scott had taken up a popular myth that handfasting was a form of trial marriage. It is not unreasonable to believe that Scott based his reference to handfasting on Pennant's

mentioning on the topic. One must also consider that Sir Walter Scott's novel was a work of fiction, therefore it isn't reliably historically accurate. However, it is in this work (The Monastery) that one can find the only reference to handfasting being a "year and a day" "we Bordermen ... take our wives, like our horses, upon trial. When we are handfasted, as we term it, we are man and wife for a year and a day: that space gone by, each may choose another mate, or at their pleasure, may call the priest to marry them for life—and this we call handfasting." A. Anton criticized Pennant for not being scholarly rigorous and being prone to romantic notions. It is also worth mentioning that the "Dictionary of Older Scottish Tongue" references a 16th century quote where no year trial is mentioned. "The said dispensacione cum nocht hayme within the said tyme..the said John the Grant is bundin..to caus thame be handfast and put togiddir..for mariage to be

The Marriage of King Arthur and Queen Guinevere by John H. Bacon

completit; Becaus..many within this toun ar handfast, as thai call it, and maid promeis of mariage a lang space bygane,.., and as yit vill nocht mary and coimpleit that honorable band,.., but lyis and continewis in manifest fornicatioun."

It is also noteworthy that within Scotland, Germanic contributions to the culture have often been downplayed in favor of their Celtic counterparts.

Namely, the Vikings were quite active in Scotland for a period, as well as the Anglo-Saxons came to influence the language and culture of the borderlands and lowland Scots.

Concluding Thoughts

As one can see, the modern Wiccan or Neopagan concept of handfasting bears little resemblance to its medieval counterpart. This does not render the ceremony invalid but simply modern in its construction. It would be intellectually dishonest if we were to continue abiding by the notion that this is an ancient Celtic custom. Instead it should be noted that it is a Germanic custom that in recent years was appropriated by the pagan community and formulated into something new.

Bibliography

Anton, A. (1958). Historical Scottish Review: Handfasting in Scotland.

Bree, H. G., Dareau, M. G., Pike, L., & Watson, H. D. (2002). A dictionary of the older Scottish tongue. Oxford: Oxford University Press.

Cowan, E. J. (2011). History of Everyday Life in Medieval Scotland.

Eska, C. M. (2010). Cáin Lánamna: An old Irish tract on marriage and divorce law. Leiden: Brill.

Howard, M. (2010). Modern Wicca: A history from Gerald Gardner to the present. Woodbury, MN: Llewellyn Publications.

Jochens, J. (1998). Women in Old Norse society. Ithaca: Cornell University Press.

Scott, W. (1913). The monastery. Boston: Houghton Mifflin.

Christopher Pinard holds a bachelor's degree in psychology, and has been doing freelance genealogy for several years. He has over a decade of experience researching Northern European mythology, folklore, and history. Follow his work on Facebook under "**Christopher Pinard - Writer** " and on Hubpages at **hubpages.com/@chrispinard**.

Courtly romance depicted on a medieval manuscript

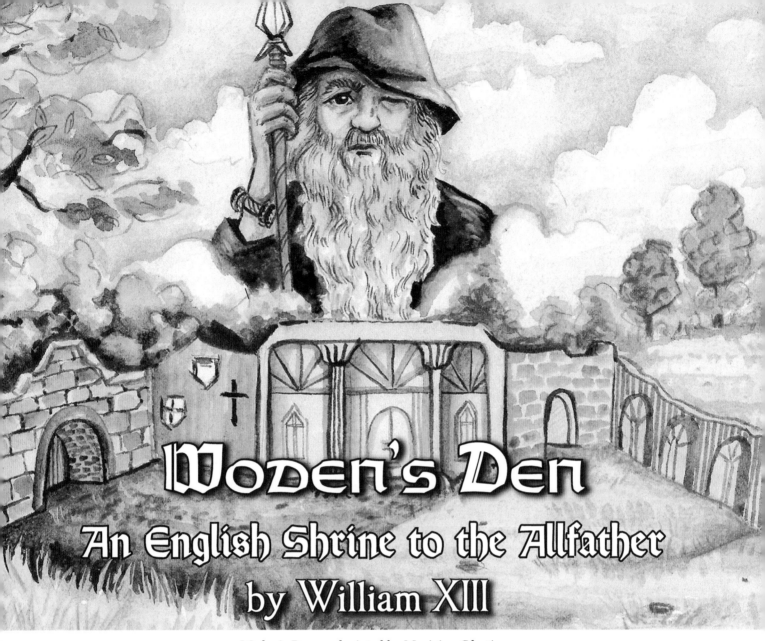

Woden's Den
An English Shrine to the Allfather
by William XIII

Woden's Den as depicted by Maricica Cârstiuc

England is home to some of the richest history in Western Europe; from Nelson's column in Trafalgar to Queen Mary I, from William the Conqueror to William of Orange, there is over a thousand years of historical bonanza that could occupy an entire library and more. A valid criticism of this history or, perhaps a by-product of the technological timeline, is that it's always streaked with an ecclesiastical flavor. The backdrop to every scene of the last 1,000 years is invariably Christianity, whilst a large bulk of English history – especially in a monarchical context – displays the Christian religion in the foreground. We often think of the struggle between Rome and King Henry VIII, or the familicide of Elizabeth I on account of religious feuding between cousins and siblings. Then there is the Civil War era, in which the Puritans under Lord Protector Oliver Cromwell, fuelled by religious zeal, outlawed practically everything of amusement – because of their Christian faith. Even the last great upheaval in English history, the so-called Glorious Revolution of 1688-89, had the struggle between Papists and Protestants at its heart.

There are two primary reasons for this; firstly, the means for actually recording history were not as adeptly developed prior to the Christianisation of the English aristocracy; secondly, the Christian ruling elite – as we shall see in more detail later on – went to great lengths to destroy or otherwise usurp any material, site or building that alluded to a time before themselves. Woden's Den in Ordsall, Greater Manchester, is a brilliant example of this; a site of rich historical and religious significance that was usurped by the Christian elite and subsequently destroyed when said elite recognized that it had much less appeal to the masses in its reconditioned format.

Woden's Den is useful to us for a number of reasons. Most importantly, it's an example of the pre-Christian heritage of the English nation, evidencing the Germanic pagan faith that was practiced here. Woden, the anglicised version of Odin, is a deity who was held in high esteem by all the Germanic peoples of Europe, representing the "chief" God for all Teutons. In Scandinavia, he's known as Odin, whilst in Germany, we find the name Wotan, derived from the proto-Germanic *wōđanaz*. One particular portal through which we can learn more about the Germanic deities is the days of the week; Wednesday is derived from the Old English *wōdnesdæg*, which later became *Wodnesday*.

In his writings, Roman historian Tacitus attested that the Germanic deity Wotan was the equivalent of Mercury. For the pagan Anglo-Saxons, Woden (could have) represented a number of things. What we know is that he was a deity of the greatest significance, and various monarchs of the Anglo-Saxon heptarchy claimed descendence from Woden as a means to justify their positions. This was, most notably, the case in the powerful kingdoms of Wessex and Mercia. In terms of what he represents, researcher Thomas Roswell has stipulated that Woden was a priestly figure who represented wisdom and a means for connecting the Pagan Saxons with that which transcends the metaphysical, as well a poet and potentially a shamanic figure. Furthermore, we know that the Pagan Saxons often made sacrifices to Woden before battle, believing that this would bring them victory. Woden also presides over Valhalla, a hall for those felled in battle, a group from which he

leads through the skies during the annual Wild Hunt.

Woden's Den was depicted and written about by Thomas Barret in 1780 as a small cave, down the lane from an ancient paved ford known as Woden's Ford. The Den is described as a naturally occurring enclave, six feet high and twenty-two yards in length, surrounded by draping foliage and decorated with 'Gothic tracery.' Barret also describes a part of the rock on which there is an inscription, which he suggests could be from the Old English runic alphabet (Elder Futhark). However, he assumes it to be the initials of Jesus the Saviour of Men (J.H.S) – unfortunately, we'll never know which assumption is correct, but both are equally plausible. This is because, as Barret and later writers have attested, Woden's Den was converted to a site of Christian site of worship at some point, although the date of this transformation is unclear. When it was an entirely Pagan site, however, it was thought to have

An illustration of the god Odin on his eight-legged horse Sleipnir, from an Icelandic 18th century manuscript

The only eye-witness rendering of Woden's Den, drawn by an observer in 1790

been a site at which offerings were made to Woden. The theory goes that travelers would visit the site prior to crossing the River Irwell and request an assurance of safe passage from the chief God. One can assume, as was the case with other Pagan rites and rituals, that the site was used for the same purpose after its Christianization – just as the alleged resurrection of Christ was conveniently placed around Easter time to coincide and absorb the Pagan festival of Ostara. The only difference in the case of Woden's Den is that "heretical" practices would be replaced by solemn prayers.

Another reason for attaching significance to Woden's Den as a historical artifact is that it offers clues towards the death or otherwise of Heathen practices in England. It is common knowledge that the Anglo-Saxon kingdoms converted to Christianity beginning in the early 7th century culminating in the last openly Pagan king being slain in 686 AD. However, the suggestion that the English population converted en masse – or willingly, for that matter – has been debunked by practically every historian researching the matter. That Woden's Den survived in the memories of local people for so long suggests that the Old Ways did not die out with the advent of Christianity. This is further supported by the heresy laws and the accompanying witch trials of the Middle-Ages. After all, if something requires a law against it, then it stands to reason the outlawed practice is still a "problem."

In the early 19th century, Woden's Den was by all accounts of great interest to antiquarians, and ordinary people still visited the site. This prompted landowner James Hall, who purchased the land in 1808, to destroy it completely so as to discourage further visitors from "trespassing" on in the area. This is typical of the British elite, especially the Christian elite, who care little for the historical significance of a place in comparison to their own comforts and preferences.

Ordsall itself, the town in which Woden's Den is located, offers other hints to England's Pagan past. For instance, there are two theories regarding the etymology of the town's name itself. The second of these theories is that the town derives its very name from Woden's Den; "*ord*" is an Old Saxon word which literally means 'primeval' or simply 'very old', whilst "*hal*" translates as 'den', giving the town's name as 'very old den' –

a reference to the holy Pagan site, perhaps? However, the town's first literary mention comes in 1177 when 'Ordeshala' paid two marks in feudal taxation, which suggests either the etymological theory is shaky or that the town's name was deliberately altered by the Christian recordkeepers as a means to eradicating the town's historic Pagan connection. Either way, this is an area of interesting speculation. There are also more contemporary references to the town's significance to the Pagan Saxons; an entire estate's street names are references to Germanic Paganism. There's Woden St, Woden's Avenue, Thor (Þunor) Grove, Freya Grove and Asgard Drive, which corresponds to the importance those three particular deities held in the Anglo-Saxon religion alongside Asgard, one of the nine worlds in Norse cosmology. It's likely that these were named by a bureaucrat with little knowledge of Pagan practices, a theory evidenced by the fact that the Norse name for Þunor was used. Nonetheless, it's a somewhat comforting reference to the Old Ways.

Woden's Den in Greater Manchester is a fantastic example of how, despite the Christianization and subsequent secularization of England, overt and covert references to pre-Christian times are all around us. This is just one example of England's beautifully Pagan past, a past all too often forgotten or otherwise expunged from the history books. Yet England does have a Pagan past, one that arguably built the very foundations of her as a nation – the Angles, Saxons, Frisians, and Jutes all brought the Old Ways to this land along with them. I invite you, the reader, to delve further into the world of Anglo-Saxon England and explore the rich Pagan history it has to offer. From place names to weekdays, festivals to local customs, hints and references are there in abundance. It's a truly interesting segment of history, and Woden's Den is just a pebble on a beach.

Bibliography and further information:

"From Runes to Ruins" (Documentary): fromrunestoruins.vhx.tv/

Hidden Manchester, "Woden's Den," hidden-manchester.org.uk

Worthington, Barry, and Graham Beech. Discovering Manchester: A Walking Guide to Manchester and Salford - Plus Suburban Strolls and Visits to Surrounding Attractions. Wilmslow: Sigma Leisure, 2002.

William XIII is an English history enthusiast. Follow him on Twitter: **twitter.com/William__XIII**

Odin depicted on a Swedish postage stamp

SKYFORGER
BALTIC HERITAGE IN SONG

An interview with Pēteris Kvetkovskis

Editor's note: Pēteris Kvetkovskis (Peter) is the lead singer, musician, and founding member of the Latvian metal band, Skyforger. His lyrics celebrate Latvian and Baltic cultural heritage with special emphasis on cultural mythology. All photos have been provided by the band.

Mythic Dawn: *I first discovered Skyforger by accident! I was searching for quick info on the Baltic Crusades, which was a Christian militant campaign against the pagan Balts resulting in genocide and destruction of culture. You had written about this topic on a blog for your band's website. So right away, your interest in cultural heritage was apparent. As I have explored your content further, I see how your Latvian and wider Baltic heritage saturates your work.*

Can you tell us what heritage means to you and why you feel it is important to incorporate it into your musical expression?

Pēteris Kvetkovskis: The thing here is I just love history; it's one of my biggest hobbies in

this life. This interest arose back in school with Ancient Greeks and Romans, but it took a while until I discovered my own past and heritage of my nation. I lived in Soviet times, when the regime tried hard to eliminate all things national. The history we were taught was full of lies and propaganda, we were educated on the idea that Latvians and other Balts were just peasants slaving for Germans until "big brother" Russia saved us. Many young people like me at those times didn't care for their own national heritage, even despised it, we lived on stories about Romans, Vikings, and North America Indians.

I came to the history of Latvia by accident, when I ran out of books to read, I got a book about an old Latvian tribe, the Semigalls, and how they fought invading German crusaders back in the 11th-13th centuries. It turned my world upside down! I saw that my ancestors were the same fierce warriors as Vikings, that we Latvians have rich and glorious history and that there is so much to discover. From that day on I knew that my work will be dedicated to spread the word about Latvian and Baltic heritage because it is still almost unknown outside our borders. The Balts are part of ancient Europe and the Indo-European nation family and yet people know Germans, Celts, Slavs but Balts still are left out, like we weren't there from the very beginning with our own culture and traditions! So it became a mission for me and Skyforger and we still keep on doing it!

I like to add here one more thing: for small nations, like Latvia, cultural, historical and traditional heritage means a lot, it is that thing which keeps the nation alive through all the hardships we endure. And that's why we cling to it so dearly!

MD: *Your album "The Battle of Saule" describes the warfare between violent Christian invaders and pagan Baltic heroes who stood boldly and strongly to defend your culture. Can you tell us why you felt it was important to tell this story? And are there any analogies from this historical period that apply to us today?*

Peter: Oh because it was an important event in our history! It was the time when our freedom was taken away. The small Baltic tribes stood against almost the whole Christian Europe, we were the last pagan bastion still holding on to our traditions. The people who fought for freedom back then are our

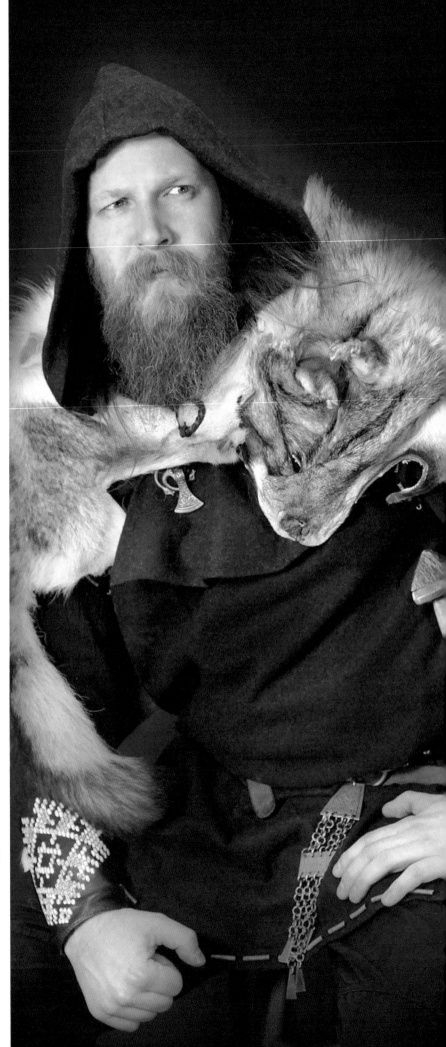

national heroes. Of course many things are glorified from those times, but nevertheless it was "a must" story to be told for our band.

You see, our history is very scarce. It was mostly written by German monks and historians, so every little thing we can discover is very important to us and it shall never be forgotten! The young Latvians must know of these historical events, because not everyone reads chronicles. I hope our music and albums help here a lot!

If we talk about analogies, then yes, there are many of them even in our late history. All our past is a constant struggle for freedom. Our small land was occupied by many big neighboring empires – Germans, Swedes, Poles, Russians, it is miracle that we, our language and culture, survived through all the centuries. Latvia became a free state only after WWI, when we finally had weapons and national troops, who brought us this freedom. And even then it was not over! Our people stood as one again before the fall of the Soviet Union and in most cases made this fall happen. So our history is one big fight for freedom and all the people who led us there are our national heroes and their stories are worth being told.

MD: *On the same album, the song "The Ancient Oak" stood out to me. The Oak was obviously an important symbol universally to Northern Europeans; Celts, Teutons, Norse, Slavs, and as your song explains, also to the Balts. The song also emphasizes our bond to the Earth. Do you have any thoughts on the Oak as a sacred symbol and the Earth-based worldview of Northern Europeans?*

Peter: The oak is a very strong pagan symbol in the whole Northern

Europe. As a big sturdy tree which lives on for hundreds of years, it became tied with gods almost in every Northern culture. The oak is a tree of thunder god, due to observation that people saw how lightning strikes it often so they had an idea that there must be something which connects thunder and oak.

In our traditional songs thunder god, Pērkuns had been seen standing by the oak or striking oak with lightning because his antagonist, god of the dead Veles, is hiding there from him in storm.

Old Prussian legends tell us about huge oak in a sacred place, Romuva, where there were statues of three gods placed near that oak or even inside its trunk and it was the main cult place for Old Prussians. People believed that gods and spirits lived inside the oaks; they brought sacrifices there in hopes that gods will protect them. Even today in our country old oaks are guarded as cultural heritage of the past and people still leave there some kind of offerings, like woven belts or colorful threads in the branches. So, yeah, it's a very strong pagan symbol!

MD: *Themes that reappear frequently in your lyrics are Latvian mythos and the Baltic gods. But your lyrics tend to be very earthy also. Elements like the sun, trees, fog, and dew are present. Reading your earthy words makes me feel your lyrics more powerfully as an experience than I would with other song lyrics. Do you think that these themes lived on more strongly in the Baltic than elsewhere in Europe? And do you think that Balts were pagan for so much longer than other Europeans plays a role in the modern Baltic experience?*

Peter: Sure it does! In this case we are lucky, because our traditions and pagan culture were left almost untouched for so many centuries. Christianity was brought here only in 11th-13th centuries, and it was brought with fire and sword. Local nobility, who turned to the new religion were quickly Germanized and lived separately from the rest of locals. The Germans who ruled the land put little effort to spread Christianity among local people, they were more interested to use those people as peasants. The churches were there, but the preaching went on in German or Latin, absolutely unknown to our people, so they stayed pagans for a long time even after official Christianization. As you can imagine all this helped a lot for old traditions to survive. They survived even until the end of 19th century when modern industrial times took it all over.

Sure, it would be foolish to say that Christianity has absolutely no impact on our culture; many traditions were forgotten or deformed by Christian dogmas, especially in later centuries when Germans finally start to preach the Bible in the Latvian language. But still, there were stories when locals, after being in church on Sunday, were seen giving offering to the old gods later the same day. Many church authorities were furious about how such things were still around, they tried to use force to stop it; like cutting down oaks, splitting stones, and even punishing people for doing it. In the end, maybe they won, but these traditions survived long enough to be part of our national culture even today!

MD: *Battle and warfare is also ever present in your lyrics. Have you chosen these themes because they pair well with the heavy metal delivery? Or do they speak to you for other reasons?*

Peter: Well, yes, it goes very well along with heavy music and without a doubt we chose those themes intentionally. But then there is this thing that almost every boy has those feelings for soldiers and warriors and glorious battles of the past. It is inside of us from birth.

But on another hand it is very bad to glorify war; it is because of this glorification more wars occurred. The new generations forget all the horrors their fathers and grandfathers went through and step in the same pool again. And it happens mostly because of glorified stories they hear in childhood, of how it all was heroic and shining, no one told them about blood, guts and suffering.

With my lyrics I try to avoid that, I tell

about simple people who got strength to endure horrors of war, about people who abandoned their normal life to sacrifice it for fight for freedom. Freedom is the main point for me here, not war or battle itself.

MD: *In other parts of the European world, or countries founded by Europeans, there is often a stigma at worst or misunderstanding at best regarding our European indigenous faith. But the Balts seem more openly accepting of their own ancient heritage. Could you tell us anything about paganism in Latvia? And has a more positive view of paganism in the Baltic region influenced the success of your band?*

Peter: As we spoke above, paganism is a part of our culture today. See, our nation didn't go through many culture revolutions and transformations like people in Western Europe did. We had no long history of writers, scientists,

painters, actors, nothing like renaissance, baroque, or neoclassical movements. So, for us it was the old traditions and the next step was the modern industrial world of the late 19th century. So this old heritage became our culture. Of course no one is worshiping the ancient gods today, but if you walk in any city in Latvia you can see national geometric signs (like swastika) all around, pagan celebrations like Summer or Winter Solstices being still widely celebrated, big choir events with people in national costumes, folk bands and folk festivals, and children are taught *Dainas* (old folk songs and rhymes) straight from childhood in kindergartens and schools. Historical places and monuments are guarded and kept. And even government supports and encourages all these activities. In today's Latvia, our old heritage and the modern world go hand in hand.

I hope at some point our band and our music has given it share to all this. At least I know many young people who got interested in Latvian history thanks to our band. So our work is not in vain!

MD: *From what I have read on Baltic nations, the people maintained more of a "dual faith" after they were forcibly converted to Christianity. People forget that although the history books might place conversion on a fixed date, that this was often only nominal and the common folk still kept their pagan beliefs and practices long after, and sometimes even into modern times. Would you say this is true of the Balts? And was this an influence on you forming a "pagan" metal band?*

Peter: Yes it's absolutely true, but I guess I already shed light on this matter in my answers above, so no point to repeat myself. As for the band itself, it is more complicated. We started to play metal music long before Skyforger. But at that time we were more interested in the Middle Ages in Central Europe - you know, King Arthur, crusaders, legend of Roland, dark mysticism, that kind of stuff. As I said it took some time till I discovered my own roots at the end of the Soviet Union. Only then was Skyforger born. So I can't say that my music was really influenced by our old tradition from the very beginnings, but I explained all this in the first of your questions.

MD: *You released a theme album as a metal rock opera called "Kurbads" based on a Latvian folk legend. Can you tell us briefly about the legend and why you felt that it was important to feature an entire album around this tale?*

Peter: Kurbads is a Latvian fairy tale/legend that survived from olden times. There were some folk enthusiasts who traveled the land and recorded all possible folk knowledge from people in the 19th century. Those tales were passed from generation to generation verbally. Among others, there were fairytales about a man who was born magically from various things (mare, iron, ox, dog, wolf, etc.), but the most common version was from a bear. This man grew up to be very strong and went out into the world to help poor people and fight evil.

I found this tale very interesting, but knowing how popular the version of the tale about Lācplēsis in Latvia, (Bearslayer - a man who was born from the bear), I took another variation (less popular but known very well) about Kurbads, son of a mare.

The whole album tells Kurbads' story: from his birth until his death in the last battle, his adventures, and his fight against his archenemy, the Snake Witch. In the tale are found very archaic topics, like a ritual of initiation, venturing into realm of dead (underworld), ancient witchcraft and magic, as well as old customs and the way of how our people saw our world. Even the act of how Kurbads was born is magical, and I thought its roots came from era of the Stone Age when people took some magical beast or god as procreator of all kin.

The idea for this album was born a long time ago, but it was left to wait while I was working on other topics. The thing is, I'm trying (at least I hope I do) to change album topics from

one album to the next, to avoid repeating myself all the time. Wouldn't it become too boring if our every album was about freedom fighting? Right? So, Kurbads came in naturally as something different than we did before and yet also representing our heritage.

MD: *I watched you perform "Kurbads" as it was acted out with actors and dancers on YouTube. As someone who values our European native culture and laments that so many others in the West do not see the value in our folklore and mythos, it made me very happy, even emotional, to see a large open air concert venue filled with Latvians cheering on the portrayal of their own heritage. You also won an award for this! The Latvian Broadcasting Media recognized your contribution to culture with their "A Kilogram of Culture" award.*

What do you think it means when other Western cultures eschew their own indigenous folkways? Does it have any effect on society? Or on individual people? Do you think that Balts may have a healthier bond to their ancient heritage than some other groups?

Peter: Yeah, it makes me sad to see things like that in Western Europe. Westerners buried their old culture themselves a long time ago. I understand that there is no one to blame today, but it all started with the collapse of Roman Empire. It was all about money and power when local chieftains invented Christianity as great tool for oppression, forced it on their own people, and with the passing centuries they tried hard to eliminate everything national and traditional that they had before. So now we are left with what we have and with deformed thinking, that your old culture is something to be ashamed of, something bad and dirty.

In this regard Baltic people have a more open-minded view on their past and culture, but it comes with all the things I said before – if we had went through the same circle as Western Europeans, the result could be the same as there.

But then again, it is only about pagan past,

Western civilization still has its own great history and traditions and stuff to be proud of! And on a positive note, I see that today people are clinging to this ancient heritage all around the world. It arouses great interest; reenactment clubs, folk and metal music, movies, books, games and so on. It's not that bad as we like to think!

MD: *Most of your music is in the heavy metal genre, but in 2003 you recorded a folk music album called Sword Song. I read that you brought in other folk musicians to record with you. And, the singing is obviously very different from the other albums. I enjoyed this album very much! Did making this album feel any different to you than the others? And do you feel differently when portraying your culture in a more traditional musical format? In other words, did more traditional music change the experience for you? Do you think you will record any other folk albums in future?*

Peter: We started to research Latvian folk music at same time we formed Skyforger. Old folk music is huge here in our country and has strong ties with our past. Many songs are very old and tell about pagan gods, rituals, and how people lived in those times. The idea here was to incorporate folk song melodies into our heavy music. Apart from that, we learned to play some old instruments and sing those songs. With folk instruments we wanted to strengthen that pagan atmosphere of our music, and the same with singing. People already can hear pure folk songs on our first demo album and it stayed that way through all the years.

At some point we learned enough of folk songs and idea to record folk album was born. Earlier we used to sing such songs at our meetings and drinking parties. Then we did a live performance at the Open Air Museum, and finally recorded the whole album. For us it was a part of what we were doing all the time, it wasn't something out of space or extraordinary because, as I said, it all started with the beginning of Skyforger.

As for another folk album, hard to say right now, time will tell… it's more because here in

Latvia we have lots and lots of folk bands and I don't know if another one in the face of Skyforger is really needed, ha ha.

MD: Thank you so much for taking the time to answer! I have been posting about Skyforger all over social media these past few weeks!

Peter: Thanks for this chance to spread a word about SKYFORGER!

More about the band, buy their music, and read their mythical lyrics translated into English on their website: **skyforger.lv/en.** And, stay up to date on their latest news and tour dates by following on Facebook: **www.facebook.com/skyforgerofficial**

Fairy Lore from the Isle of Skye

By Carolyn Emerick

Fairies dancing on water by August Malmström

For many hundreds of years, Skye remained an island largely isolated from the rest of Scotland. It did not exist in a complete vacuum, as it was settled by both Celts and Norse, and probably by the Picts before them. But, there were always comings and goings by way of ships and boats from the mainland and abroad. Due to this sea access, Skye became a Viking hot spot, like so many of the other Scottish Isles. Its isolation became more pronounced toward the Industrial Revolution. As mechanized farming equipment, rail roads, and eventually motorways became the norm across mainland Britain, residents of Skye continued using traditional farming methods and modes of transport, making the island somewhat of a time capsule. It is no wonder, then, that fairy lore lingered on after it had begun to erode elsewhere.

Life moved at a slower pace in Skye and stories of fairies continued to be passed on orally. Storytelling is, after all, a form of entertainment that comes with no technology necessary. Author Mary Julia MacCulloch recorded some folklore during her time in Skye, which was published in the journal "Folklore" in 1922. She says that nearly all of her stories were collected from in and around the village of Portree.

Yet, when it comes to Skye, the precise location of her interviews made little difference. She explains that the island was a tight-knit community and the inhabitants were a hearty breed of folk. It was not uncommon to see an elderly woman walking twenty-six miles just to attend mass. Many inhabitants belonged to parishes at distances quite far from where they lived. These people, who were so used to hard work, thought nothing of traversing their island on foot. As such, folk stories traveled throughout the island with ease.

It is amusing that Ms. MacCulloch laments the fact that the youths of the island read nothing but newspapers and novellas. She blames their lack of knowledge of local lore and legend on their reading habits. Today we might dance a jig if we caught our teenagers reading the newspaper!

MacCulloch gives further background on Skye island life when she explains that most inhabitants spoke only Gaelic so she had difficulty communicating with them. In research for other articles, I have explored the use of Germanic languages such as Norn and Scots, derivatives of Old Norse and Old English respectively, on the eastern Scottish Isles. Skye has an element of Norse heritage, just as Orkney and Shetland do. But, the Scottish Isles in the North Sea retained greater Norse influence while the isles to the west retained a greater Celtic influence.

Mary Julia MacCulloch mentions that themes in fairy lore tend to be universal regardless of location. This is true in many of the stories she shares. We see many of the usual stories such as a beautiful human child taken by the fairies and replaced by a sickly, ugly changeling. Also mentioned are stories of people being taken into the mounds for what seems like a few hours, but days or years have passed when then re-emerge.

Another motif recognizable from such well-known stories as "Rumpelstiltskin" is the fairies doing manual labor for their human counterparts. This is also seen in another famous

German fairy tale, "The Shoemaker and the Elves." The lowland Scots equivalent to such helpful creatures are the brownies. As it happens, the fairies on the island of Skye have a penchant for helping make tweed. In fact, Harris Tweed is a local company still manufacturing traditional fabrics on Skye.

Well, tweed making by hand on Skye pre-dates the industrial age and, according to lore, may have been aided by the fairies. MacCulloch's interviews reveal that some Skye crofters desired to spin and weave the very tweed that their island

became so famous for, but they became too tired. Under the influence of exhaustion, the would-be tweeders made the mistake of wishing aloud (so that the fairies could hear them) that the tweed would just be finished. Overhearing this wish, the fairies appeared and demanded the necessary tools to finish the chore.

Industrious were these fairies, indeed. For, they would not leave when the task was completed. The crofters were forced to seek the help of a wise man. He advised them to direct the fairies to build a roof, but that

Art by John Anster Fitzgerald

the roof must be made of a special kind of wood. There only existed one tree on the entire island made of the kind of wood needed. When the fairies began their building, they were unable to complete it. And so, they were had no choice but to leave the crofters to their own devices, as they were before.

Sometimes, a human could be called to do a favor for the fairies. One such person was a midwife of Skye. This particular midwife also tended her own small herd of cows. One night she went out to call the cows home when she was approached by a fairy man. He bid her to follow him. She refused, saying she had to tend to her cows. The fairy man insisted that if she helped him, her cows would be well looked after. When she arrived in his fairy home, she found that his wife was having difficulties in childbirth. The situation was so dire that the delivery and subsequent health concerns of mother and child took several days of care. By the time her services were no longer needed, eight full days had gone by! When the midwife returned to her own home, however, she found that the fairy man had been true to his word. Her cattle never could have been better cared for in her absense.

Another fairy story from Skye comes to us from K.M. Briggs who published a few decades later, also in "Folklore" journal. She received the story from the wife of a minister from the Isle of Skye. As the story goes, a little boy and his sister had been left to stay with their grandmother while their mother went to nurse an ailing friend some distance away. A neighbor boy joined the pair to play. After a pleasant afternoon of playing in the sunshine, the children began to feel tired and a little ornery.

An elderly woman happened to call on the children's grandmother. Now, this woman was known to be a "wise woman," and had an idea about how to cheer up these bairns. This wise woman took a liking to the children and asked if they would like to see something special. They replied that yes, they would, so she beckoned them to follow her. What happened next is reminiscent of Irish poet William Allingham's most

Loch Coruisk, Isle of Skye, by Sidney Richard Percy, 1874

famous poem,

The Fairies:

Up the airy mountain,
Down the rushy glen,
We daren't go a-hunting
For fear of little men; The

Wee folk, good folk,
Trooping all together;
Green jacket, red cap,
And white owl's feather!

Down along the rocky shore
Some make their home,
They live on crispy pancakes

Of yellow tide-foam;

Some in the reeds
Of the black mountain-lake,
With frogs for their watch-dogs,
All night awake.

The children followed the old woman down a winding path through a glen and over to a little burn. Following her instructions, the children held hands, the first with the wise woman and so on so that all four were connected. Then, they sat down beside the

stream. Suddenly, on the other side of the brook the children beheld an iridescent fire burning in twilight of the early evening. They couldn't believe their eyes when fairies appeared around the fire! The fairies were bedecked all in green and danced merrily about the flames. When the children arrived by the very same burn the next day to show their friends, the fairies were nowhere to be seen.

K.M. Briggs reveals that the little boy was the husband of the woman who told her this story. According to his wife, the minister reckoned it was the presence of the wise woman that allowed the children to see the fairies. By holding the hand of the witch, and all children connecting together in a line, the minister thought each child was able to tap into the energy or extra sense that the wise woman carried. For it was said among the villagers that this woman possessed the famous Celtic "second sight."

The fairies of Skye turn up in the island's beautiful landscape as well as its lore. There are many landmarks that are associated with tales of stories. And some that seem to have earned their association for their otherworldly appearance rather than any legend. The fairy pools of Skye are one such example. These are naturally occurring pools typically under waterfalls, usually with very clear water, unique rock formations, and surrounded by vivid color. These pools are often graced with an abundance

The Enchanted Piper by William Holmes Sullivan

The fairy pools of Skye as depicted by Vasilios Markousis

of minerals and decorated with beautiful blue-green algae which give them a reputation as places of healing.

This phenomenon is also seen with the holy wells all over Britain, Ireland, and Europe. These were typically fresh water springs with similar properties. In most cases, these wells and springs were sacred to pagans long before the Christianization of Europe. After conversion, however, the Church adopted them as holy wells. A similar instance is seen in Bath, England. The famous hot springs of Bath are thought to have been a holy site to British pagans. The Romans, always one with a keen eye for opportunity, harnessed the naturally heated mineral water when they built a traditional Roman bath around it.

Skye is just one of many examples of locales which preserved the folklore of the Europeans who populated the region. These stories are elements that give Europe its own unique culture and they serve to demonstrate a living mythic tradition in the minds of the local people. We see quite well that our indigenous folkways lived on and were passed down into recent memory. It is crucially important not to let this flame be extinguished now.

Bibliography:

Briggs, K. M. (1961). Some Late Accounts of the Fairies. Folklore, 72 (3), 509-519.

MacCulloch, Mary Julia (1922). Folk-Lore of the Isle of Skye. Folklore, 33 (2), 201-214.

Swire, Otta F. (1961). Skye: The Island and its Legends. London: Blackie & Son Limited.

Carolyn Emerick is the editor of Mythic Dawn and Europa Sun magazines. She has a bachelor's degree in literature, graduate level training in archival studies, and has been studying European cultural heritage for most of her life. See her work at **CarolynEmerick.com.**

Dreams of Ydalir:
A Mythological Fantasy

by Jenn Campus
Illustrations by Roberto Campus

"Dreams of Ýdalir" is an illustrated historical fantasy heavily based on European mythology and our own personal relationships with the Gods of our home and hearth. The story centers around the Gods Wuldor (also known as Ullr) and Elen of the Ways, and aims to tell their untold myths. Very little is known about either of these enigmatic figures, but through over a decade of personal research and working directly with the Gods, I have been able to patch together what is known about them and what I have learned, to create a rich tapestry, including fundamental truths spoken by the Gods themselves to help us humans understand our own place in the cosmos.

I write this story and Roberto illustrates it, in an attempt to facilitate the return of the Old Gods into the everyday lives of their people through adding beauty, richness, and relatability to the old tales, often based on translations written by early Christian monks which can be very dry in content. We make the stories more relatable by telling part of the story through our human heroine, 17-year-old Fawn, and other parts of the story from the perspective of the Gods themselves. Then we package it all in a beautiful format with amazing sketches and illustrations to bring the words to life.

Every writer needs an amazing illustrator, and every illustrator longs for the stories behind their images to be told. From the beginning we knew that the visual component would have to be as compelling as the story itself. Roberto is the most talented artist I know and he has listened to my stories about Wuldor and Elen for years, so he knows them intimately and has really brought them and the other characters in the book alive. He had a career creating illustrations for many famous publishers like Marvel and DC Comics, the Game of Thrones and War of Warcraft TCGs, as well as Dungeons and Dragons and Gurps, so he has an immense passion for the fantasy genre.

By the end of the project we hope to have a collection of beautiful portraits of the various Gods featured in the story, like Thor, Freyja, Idunna, Odin, and Sif in addition to the main divine characters, Wuldor and Elen, and will likely add a line of prayer/devotional cards to our offerings.

We describe our story "where Norse Mythology and Mists of Avalon meet," as my writing is heavily influenced by European mythology and my love for the legends of King Arthur. Since I am a folklorist, and spend a great part of my life writing about culinary anthropology, I always look for ingenious ways to bring together my favorite fiction and nonfiction genres when I write. So my work always has elements of fantasy/mythology, culinary arts,

DREAMS of YDALIR

ritual, the magical arts, history and the many uses of herbs.

Synopsis

Our story is based in a rich world where mythology and fantasy meet. The year is 1794, Fawn is a seventeen-year-old orphaned girl living in the Scottish lowlands. When she begins having strange dreams of a flame-haired woman named Elen who appears to be part human, part deer and Wuldor, a mysterious dark-haired woodsman who gifts her with a magical deer mask that allows her to travel to other worlds, she believes she has the resources to finally find her own fey-touched mother. As her relationship with these mythical beings deepens, she writes it all down in her journal and sketches some of the pivotal moments in her life. Through this coming of age tale, she is gifted with the divine stories of the Gods, and learns her true origins. "Dreams of Ýdalir" tells about a world that exists beneath the veil of our own familiar world. It is a world you will love getting lost in.

This project is a labor of love and

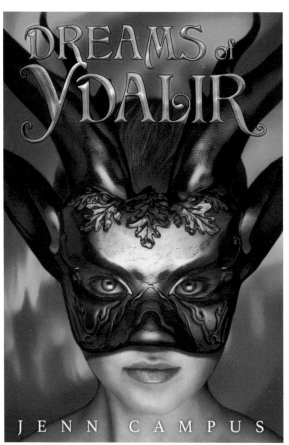

58

devotion to the old ways. We rely completely on funding from individuals. The production of "Dreams of Ýdalir" is lovingly supported by our Patreon supporters who range from fantasy fiction and art fans, Pagans and Norse mythology buffs ,to comic book readers, young adults, and those people who love strong female leads.

If you are dedicated to the old ways and want to see our Gods more present in modern life, we will love your support. Also if you love fiction, fantasy art, and Northern European mythology, you will love "Dreams of Ýdalir." Subscribe today on Patreon to join us on this fantastical journey through the halls of Asgard and find out the secrets of the Otherworld!

If you subscribe before the end of August, send us a note after you subscribe and let us know you found us through Mythic Dawn we will send you the current issue plus *all back issues* the first month! Normally, new subscribers start with the first issue and each month get the subsequent issue. So you will get a ton of value from the start! Thank you.

Find us and subscribe to Dreams of Ýdalir

Patreon: **www.patreon.com/dreamsofydalir**

Facebook: **www.facebook.com/dreamsofydalir**

Dreams of Ýdalir Blog: **dreamsofydalir.com**

Jenn Campus Author: **jenncampusauthor.com**

The Art of Roberto Campus: **www.robertocampus.com**

DREAMS of YDALIR

WE ARE THE WAVE MAIDENS:

Folklore's Forgotten Frauleins

BY JULEIGH HOWARD-HOBSON

Mermaids by Karl Wilhelm Diefenbach

We understand quite calmly, despite the fact that none of us can stay still for long, that our names, our natures, our very existences are quite unknown to most of the world now. Out here, where we splash, where we glitter, where we well or swell...there is not much human interaction anymore. Those halcyon days of renown are so very far from us, here in the waves of great grey beasts which neither see or hear us, and certainly never suspect we are about. Even worse are the flying ships that take humans from shore to shore without ever so much as the tiniest bit of our oceans ever touching their journeys. Unfair, unfair we cry. We could wave, but why would we? They wouldn't notice, and if they did, no one of us could ever reach up high enough to pull them under...

Does anyone understand our position? Understand how unfair this position is? We are not unaware of what goes on above the water's skin. Our race is not unknown. Frigga, Odin, Thor, even the chaotic Loki are names, not only remembered, but actively being spoken as we splash unknown... Furthering the indignity, everyone has heard at least *something* about *Frey* and *Freya*, those insufferably land-locked twin children of the sea god *Njord*, who are considered the Lord and Lady of the earth... la di da. With the exception of *Thor*, they are the most popular offspring of the Northern Gods. Indeed, more of Freya's myths have come down to us than any other female deity's have. We put it down to her witchcraft, but it doesn't matter in the end. Our divine ways cannot compete.

So much less familiar are we, the daughters of the Norse Lord, *Aegir*, who with our mother, *Ran,* rules the seas and all the creatures in them. Not Norse gods, no no... we are not members of the airy *Aesir* or the earthy *Vanir*, we are the final watery third of the divine trinity; our parents are omnipotent and we are divine in our own rights.

In the way of our folk, where names are more than just something to call a body by, Aegir's name means ocean, and Ran's means robber. Fitting names, for our father once granted sailors safe passage upon his waters (while they believed in him, that is, he takes little interest these days), while our mother preferred to rob those same sea faring ships with a perfectly vast net, happily pulling any number of drowned men down into the murky depths. Sailors called being dragged to the bottom of the ocean as being dropped in 'Aegir's Wide Jaws' and for this insult, Ran never left one live. Thinking back, perhaps if she had, the name would have changed, allowing all seafaring men to know exactly whose jaws they were that would snap them from their world of air and land... but mother was not what we would call temperate...

We have one brother. The fact that he is the only son, and this era being patriarchal, you would think he would be yet lauded and held high in memory as the sole male heir to an oceanic throne that covers all the earth's water...but no, like us he has faded. Unlike us, though, his name is used every day, his presence felt all over the world, wherever there is water and moving air. He is Wind, and he blows across our shore-bound world from pole to pole, strand to strand... never settling, never calming. We love him, but his nature, like mother's, is far too quick to change for any meaningful relationship to be held closely, if it is to be held dearly.

Not that we cannot handle him! There are nine of us. We were once known as the Wave Maidens, some called us the Billow Maidens, either way we are the original daughters of the sea. Mermaids have traded on our coin for time eternal - those vile, fish smelling, stringy haired hybrids – basking in tales of our beauty, our blue eyes, our long fine blonde hair and our blue and white fineries which are constantly attributed to them. We are disgusted by mer-dom's female wretches, they are not divine, they possess no magic, no ability besides stealing our reputation, and when they die - for they die, unlike us - they stink to the highest of the nine worlds.

We are nothing like mermaids, we are everything they wish to be.

Himinglæva is our fairest sister, she can appear as a wave transparent enough that you may see Sol the sun shining

Water nymph by Gaston Brussiere

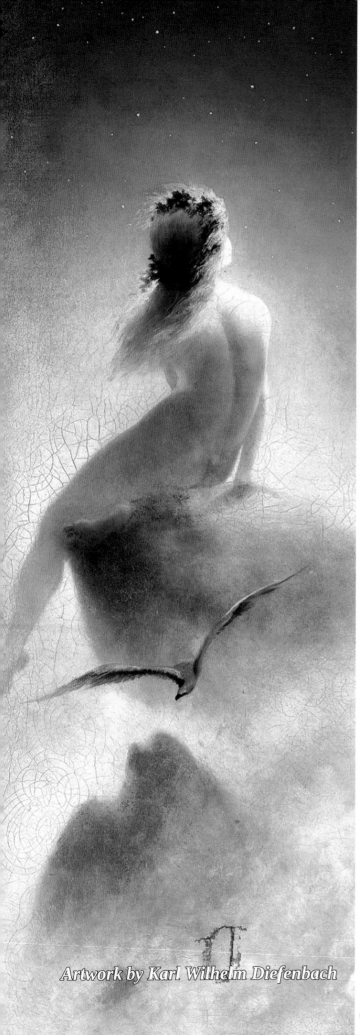

through her. Sailors have long fallen in love with her long blonde hair, her draped shimmery blue beauty. Should these sea men try rowing their small boats out toward her...they are likely to be suddenly confronted by another sister, the ever agitated *Dufa*, whose jealousy of Himinglaeva takes the aspect of the pitching action of waves. Down they go, the confused wretches, drowning as they look to transparent gloriousness, heaved from their boats as they reach out, not knowing that it is Dufa whose offended arms shall embrace them forever...or until she grows weary.

Hefring is our golden haired one, she comes forth as waves that rise from the surface, rippling with laughter, sunshine tippled and sometimes warm. If she is in the mood, she will catch Dufa's victims before they fatally plunge, and safely bring them over to Himingleava, who never tires of male appreciation and may even take them home with her if *Bylgja* doesn't interrupt. Byligja is the tallest of us, she is the billowing waves; the ocean currents obey her command. Should she decide that any seaman is worth a closer look, the ocean will bring him to her. She doesn't often care, though, preferring to play at the water surface, draping herself upon rocks, calling to our airy brother to obey her watery directives. Sea spray is the usual result of inconsequential disagreements between them, while typhoons come from those more deeply set squabbles to which two such divine commanders are prone. Alas!

How much nicer is little curly haired *Udr* - she can be found in the bubbling, frothing waves that tickle the edges of the sea shores to the delight of crabs, gulls and humans alike. Like Hefring, she can be warm, but she never takes lives, never threatens livelihoods, no matter how far she pulls away from the strand. She is thin, pretty, capricious and by far the happiest of us. She basks in the glories of splashes, in shell strewn mornings, in tide pools, in slowly lingering across sun warmed stretches of sugar-like beach grain... She is the princess of every sand castle.

She gets along the best with our tow-headed sister *Dröfn*, whose presence is known as long curling sea waves, the combers that break just before the shore. Together they hug the edges of our world, rising to taste the air, reaching to touch the earth - mostly through them we connect with the Aesir and Vanir, completing the holy triplicity which is divine existence. They are the best spirits humanity can find among us, the *Billow Maidens*. Throw a coin into the sea, and they will gladly reciprocate with gifts from the ocean.

Be careful, though, when you throw that coin, lest you awaken *Hrönn* from her deep sleeps, for she brings no gladness, no gift but that of sucking rip tides, of water that pulls and drags, of pressure that builds and, eventually, death far, far below the roof of our world. Even Wind despairs of her tendencies to invert the natural order, for she has taken him down further than he would like on more than one occasion - she cannot offset his buoyancy, although she gravely tries. And will not think twice to hold what she has pulled. No souls leave her company once they enter into it.

Better, far better, to be a guest of *Blódughadda* - for although she appears as the bloody waves that follow sea battles and land-edged massacres, she does not keep what she touches. Indeed, she merely carries forth the scarlet tinged results of human action and interaction, playing with every mortal's life blood as it runs through human fingers as well as hers. She is the most frightening of us, although the least likely to ever appear. Particularly these days, although she still does enjoy

The Nereides by Gaston Bussiere

the occasional cargo-ship disaster. No one seems to enjoy her back, though. She combs her long red hair, water-thinned blood dripping from her slender fingertips, and doesn't care at all.

Kolga doesn't care for much, either. The icy waves of polar seas and winter seasons are her cold aspects. Pale blue eyes set in snow white skin, her pale—almost white—hair hangs stiff and frozen, breaking audibly as she tosses her cold head in disdain. All who

encounter her perish as though charmed to stone by her glacial beauty. Medusa, that Greek gorgon who wishes she could be one of us, recounts Kolga's petrifying magic, although without the cold beauty or the water of our icy hearted ninth sister.

Not all who encounter us think that most of us are perilous—Odin himself found us sleeping on the sand and fell enthralled. From this enrapture, divine and complicated, emerged one son - *Heimdallr*.

Our son. As is fitting for a magical creation of water and air, Heimdallr guards *Bifrost*, the rainbow bridge that spans between *Midgard* and *Asgard* (or as you would have it now, earth and the heavens).

More important to humanity than to our race, Heimdallr is also the ancestor of mankind itself, having ventured forth and fathered the three social classes of man (peasants / thralls, farmers & craftsmen / karls, nobility / earls); making us each your grandmother. Your epoch holds that human origins may lie in the briny sea... and for once, your science got something utterly right.

We have always existed. We are the Wave Maidens, Norse mothers of the father of the human race. Come, children, the depths are waiting. Now you know our names. Learn our ways.

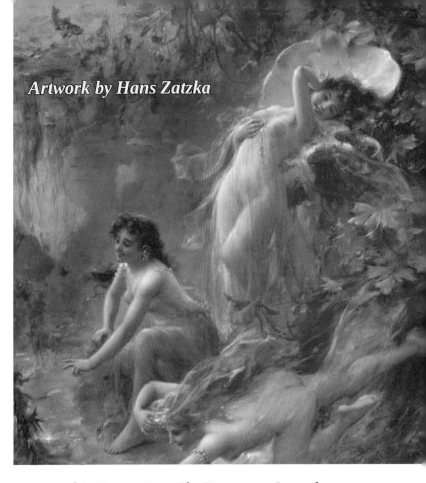

Artwork by Hans Zatzka

Juleigh Howard-Hobson's numinous works have appeared in Europa Sun, The Runestone Journal, Heathen Call, Northern Traditions, Hex Magazine, The Occidental Quarterly, Faerie Magazine, Enchanted Conversation, From the Roaring Deep and Daughter of the Sun (both from Bibliotheca Alexandria), Mandragora (Scarlett Imprint) and many other places, including a series of articles on European folk traditions for the Manticore Press website. She has four books out, among them the The Cycle of Nine (Ravenshalla Press). She has been nominated for "The Best of the Net" and The Pushcart Prize (twice) and is currently nominated for a Rhysling Award.

Heimdallr by Emil Doepler

The Green Man
& the Survival of Our
Folk Soul
by Carolyn Emerick

Green Man by Maricica Cârstiuc

Much has been said about the destruction of European culture by forced assimilation into Abrahamic ideology by the elites over the centuries. There is, of course, a strong parallel with the elite-driven forced erosion of our culture and the demographic replacement of ethnic-Europeans in Western society today. It is fair and right to make these observations and feel not only concern, but also alarm, at the pace at which we see the powers that be directing the erasure of Western cultural heritage. However, it would be wrong to end our saga with that chorus. Indigenous European

culture has, indeed, survived the attacks levied at us in the past, so there is a great deal of reason to believe that we can weather this current onslaught and survive as an ethnic group. To understand this, one needs only to look into the magical realm of the European folk tradition. For, it is there, in the misty and ethereal realm of *Faerie,* where we see the heartbeat of our own *Folk Soul* living on. This collective soul that we all share as an ethno-culture has never died. But, its sound has certainly been muted in recent decades. Therefore, the onus is on us, as individuals and together as an ethnic group, to blow off the

dust and turn the key still set in the rusty old padlock that guards the treasures of our own cultural past. Once the treasure chest is opened, many shining gems are waiting to be found. One, in particular, has been waiting centuries to be our guide. He is known today as the Green Man.

The Green Man serves as somewhat of a mascot, if you will, for the tenacious spirit of the European Folk Soul for many reasons. While his image seems to date back to time immemorial, the name by which he is known now is very recent. His face graces the walls, ceilings, corners, buttresses, and columns of Christian churches found far and wide across Western Europe. The earliest examples of the Green Man as a motif in English churches date to the 12th century, but there are much older examples on the European continent. Art historians had traditionally referred to the motif as "foliate heads," due to the leafy foliage that bedecks the human face. His resurrection in the modern mind as "Green Man" did not occur until the 20th century when interest in our indigenous past could finally find some breathing space thanks to the fortuitous weakening of the Christian choke-hold on Western society. References to green men in earlier historical sources are rare, though they do exist. There are a few scattered references recorded in the Elizabethan Era that mention "green men."

Interpretations of what these green men symbolize vary. There is a strong trend to be dismissive of interpretations that assert pagan origins to folk traditions when the evidence trail leads to no smoking gun. However, for a variety of reasons, evidence *will* be sparse. This is due to many factors; from the cold and damp climate found in much of Europe which accelerates the decomposition of organic materials to organized and targeted destruction campaigns. There is no historical document that says "look, these green men seen here in churches are a representation of the same spirit of the woodland that we see mimicked in costume by revelers dancing in folk festivals." But, we all possess a pair of eyeballs and, presumably, a brain equipped with the ability to look at these dancing green men bedecked

A Green Man in stained glass in a church located in the village of Pennal, Gwynedd, North Wales

in leafy foliage as they participate in folk traditions that have been occurring at least as long as anyone has been observing and recording European culture and see a strong similarity between them and the "foliate heads" that are found in European churches far and wide.

Many observers and researchers have made this connection and asserted quite strongly that the Green Man is an overt pagan symbol, perhaps even a deity, that lived on in the folk consciousness of Europeans well into the modern era. In their book, "Gargoyles & Grotesques: Paganism in the Medieval Church," Ronald Sheridan and Anne Ross assert that not only green men, but other fantastical figures found throughout medieval cathedrals are evidence of a living pagan

tradition. Indeed, I have strongly argued that Christianity was simply a political ideology pushed for the benefit of the elites in power, but in terms of the beliefs of the people themselves, Christianity was a veneer on the surface under which lies a deep cavern wherein our own native faith still thrived.

Green men in churches can vary in appearance. Some appear benign, gentle, and kind, while others seem frightening, hostile, and snarling. Some have interpreted these "foliate heads" to symbolize the forces of nature which can, themselves, be both kind and cruel. Others have believed the foliage surrounding the human face to symbolize fertility and, thus, human sexuality. This interpretation tends to assert that these foliate heads are present in Christian

churches to demonstrate the Abrahamic conquest and suppression of our human carnal desires. However, as before, there is no documentation to point to from the past to explain what the imagery means or why it was placed in the churches. Indeed, if there were some medieval document written by a church cleric, the information would be heavily laden with Abrahamic bias. For instance, many Irish sources insist that fairies originated as angels who fell from heaven and were damned to exist somewhere between heaven and hell. Any mythologist understands that this idea originated as an attempt to Christianize indigenous European spirituality and ascribe a foreign biblical meaning to native supernatural entities that were still very real in the consciousness of the

18th century print of chimney-sweeps' on May Day dressed as Jack in the Green in London

people. Yet, some folklorists still discuss this as the "origin" of fairies. I find this asinine. We cannot expect to understand the meaning of indigenous folk belief if we are taking at face value the definitions recorded by the very people who were working with an overt agenda to obliterate these folk beliefs from living memory.

To assume a connection between these foliate heads in churches and the green men who still appear at European folk festivals as men in costumes made up of green foliage (the most famous character being Jack in the Green), seems quite obvious.

Artwork on the sign for the Green Man, King's Stag, Dorest, England. Photo by Trish Steel

A foliate head in the shape of an acanthus leaf on Bamberg cathedral, Germany, early 13th century

To connect them with fertility of both the earth and human beings is an apt interpretation when one studies the other symbols and customs that are traditional to the European holiday lexicon. Green Man fits snugly in context with other overt imagery of both animal and vegetable fertility that still pervades our holidays today. The most likely meaning, and I say this built upon many years of studying the folk tradition of Europe, is that he symbolizes that liminal juncture between mankind and the natural world, hearkening back to the time when we, too, were as wild as the animals. This interpretation is strengthened by the fact that the "Jack in the Green" tradition bleeds into the "wild man" archetype. Far and wide across Europe today, clustered strongly in the Alpine region

but still occurring widespread in various European locales, men bedecked in shabby coats of fur, straw, branches, and/or leaves prance throughout the town on parade during certain regional festivals. The Wild Man himself deserves more attention than we can give him here. Sufficed to say that there are a variety of theories regarding his origin and meaning, but almost all of them point to some kind of earlier stage in the development of mankind, be it an evolutionary stage, representing our past as hunter gatherers, or even some archane human species.

In all stages of human development, that is, until the Industrial Age broke us from our ties to the rhythms and cycles of life, humankind was deeply aware of nature. We understood the meaning of

European "Wild Men" fighting North African blackamoors on a 14th century tapestry

fertility. We knew that our sustenance and survival was dependent on both the fertile earth as well as our own ability to repopulate our society. It might well be said that the crux of indigenous European "religion" was not simply "earth-based," solar or lunar cults, or any other definition more so than a literal *fertility* cult. When Abrahamism was imposed upon the populace from the top-down, it could not break the embedded understanding in our cultural consciousness of the inherent importance of fertility. Literally everything depended upon it. So, we see that just as churches sprung up on sites that had already been sacred to Europeans under our own native worldview, it seems quite clear

that churches purposefully brought sacred imagery from our pagan past into Christian places of worship.

It must be remembered that Christian imagery is inherently foreign to the European lexicon. We are not people whose culture formed among desert nomads. We, for the most part, were settled people. While there are some notable differences between Northern and Southern Europeans, neither group's lifestyle bore any resemblance to that which is described in the Bible. And, especially for Europeans of the North, we were very much people of the forest. The same archetypal-spirit thread that

emanates from the Green Man is seen in other figures that emerged in later stages of society, such as both the Robin Hood and Peter Pan characters. The color green is strongly figured into both. Whereas Robin Hood is synonymous with a "wild" man living outside of the dictates of society and off the land in the forest, Peter Pan's association with both youth and an otherworld bring to mind notions of supernatural regeneration of life.

Although the Green Man has not been well known by this particular name until more recently in time, he was not unknown to his people. Do we need hard evidence to understand that which speaks to the soul? And, I do not mean the "soul" in the Abrahamic sense. No, I mean, squarely, our Folk Soul. That is, the collective spiritual force that resides in each one of us by virtue of the blood of kinship that flows through our veins. Try as they might, the elites have not been able to rend the European Folk Soul asunder. That the Green Man made a massive resurgence in popularity concurrently with the rejection of Christianity and rise of "neo-pagan" religions like Wicca should not in any way diminish his meaning as something very ancient, powerful, and *living*.

The Green Man lives. He lives in you, he lives in me, and he lives in every single one of us who has ever sat under the trees of the forest and breathed in the life-force found therein. The beautiful culture of our forefathers and foremothers may be faltering. Indeed, it must be acknowledged that it is wounded and hurting. And, so, it may be no coincidence that we see the Green Man spring back to life in the European consciousness today. We need his life-force now more than ever before.

Green Man by Maricica Cârstiuc

Bibliography and Further Reading:

Lindahl, Carl, John McNamara and John Lindow. Medieval Folklore. Oxford: Oxford University Press, 2002.

Rose, Carol. Spirits, Fairies, Leprechauns, and Goblins: An Enclyclopedia. New York: W. W. Norton & Co, Inc., 1996.

Ross, Ronald Sheridan and Anne. Gargoyles & Grotesques: Paganism in the Medieval Church. Boston: New York Graphic Society, 1975.

Roud, Jacqueline Simposon and Steve. A Dictionary of English Folklore. Oxford: Oxford University Press, 2000.

Simpson, Jacqueline. European Mythology. London: The Hamlyn Publishing Group, 1987.

Carolyn Emerick is the editor of Mythic Dawn and Europa Sun magazines. She has a bachelor's degree in literature, graduate level training in archival studies, and has been studying European cultural heritage for most of her life. See her work at **CarolynEmerick.com**.

Submissions:

We are seeking writers and artists who are passionate about celebrating and promoting European cultural heritage with a focus on mythology, folklore, legend, and European Native Faith. **The magazine is unable to pay for contributions**, but we WILL promote your work:

- We will give all contributors a byline mentioning their website, blog, books, projects, and/or anything the individual wishes to promote.
- All contributors will receive two printed copies of the issue they feature in. In addition, they will receive a digital copy in PDF with permission to share with close friends and family.

We are seeking the following types of content:

Primarily we are seeking informational researched articles discussing mythology and folklore.

- This type of article should be approx 1250 to 3500 words.
- **Please do not use footnotes. Citations are not required**, but if apt, please use MLA style in-text citations (a great guide is on the Purdue Owl website).
- Please DO include a bibliography of at least three sources.

Personal essays pertaining to European Native Faith (paganism, Heathenry, etc) are accepted.

- These should be approx 750-1500 words, no bibliography required.
- Essays on how mythology touched your life personally fall under this category.
- Personal accounts of folkloric traditions you've experienced and participated in would also be welcome.

We do not accept fiction, but will consider fictionalized retellings of myth, folklore, legend. However, due to space constraints we experience with print-on-demand format, length is a concern. This genre will also need to be **capped at approx 2500 words**.

Poetry on myth, folklore, legend, etc is welcome. Generally speaking, we prefer traditional poetry comprised of form, rhyme, and meter.

Original art by artists who are inspired by these topics is especially welcome.

All contributors please include a byline with your submission. This is a short few sentences about the author or artist. This is where you can share your background, education, and plug your website, blog, book, project, etc.

Please send submissions and inquiries to MythicDawnMag@gmail.com.

Printed in Great Britain
by Amazon

36782751R00043